The ReExamined Life:
What is Possible After Job Loss?

Bill Van Steenis
with Greg Smith

D1468366

Black Lake Press
TELL YOUR STORY
BLACKLAKEPRESS.COM

The ReExamined Life

THIS BOOK IS DEDICATED TO MY WIFE BARBARA
WHO MARRIED ME FOR RICHER AND POORER,
FOR BETTER AND WORSE
AND IN SICKNESS AND IN HEALTH.
WE HAVE EXPERIENCED ALL OF THESE
IN THE PAST TWENTY-FIVE YEARS AND OUR
MARRIAGE IS STRONGER THAN EVER.

WITH LOVE,

BILL

❧ Contents ᗗ

❧ Acknowledgments ❦

As a first time writer I have many people to thank who have believed in me and helped me through this process.

First, I need to thank my wife Barbara, my friend and partner in life. It has been Barb who has believed in me enough to trust me with every cent of our savings and then some to produce more than one project that never flew. She has also supported me in every ministry idea I have ever had including giving away the money we had saved for our taxes and for allowing me to travel to dangerous destinations like Haiti and Africa. This book is dedicated to you.

My daughter Jennifer had to sacrifice

time with her father and she never complained when I spent hundreds of hours working, writing scripts and producing programs. She too sacrificed for my dreams. Thanks Scoob for your love, support and understanding.

My parents Ross and Betty van Steenis have taught me much. My dad taught me the value of work and the importance of doing everything with excellence. He also taught me the importance of valuing and protecting my personal reputation. My mother Betty has loved and encouraged me all my life and stood by me and believed in me as only a mother can believe in a son. For that love and support I will be forever grateful. Thanks Mom.

My business partner and sister-in-law Angela Schut has been a great friend and co struggler in a wild and crazy business. My wife likes to say, "Angela is the softer side of Bill." Those of you who know me know that's true. Angela has forced me to learn to think before I speak....most of the time. Thank you Angela for your thousands of hours of working side by side with me for the same common goal, to always deliver our clients more than they expected and to make everyone we come in contact with feel better about themselves than when they met us.

My dear friend and co-author Greg Smith did a masterful job of weaving my thoughts and ideas together in a cohesive work that has become *The ReExamined Life*. Without Greg's extraordinary skills, hard work and dedication to this project it would not have been possible. Thanks Greg for your vision and dedication to this work. I'm looking forward to our next book together.

I also need to thank my business partner Steve Pennington who worked on the manuscript with me, wrote video scripts, directed our video products and who spent hundreds of hours working with me on our original project the *Winning Choices Reemployment System* back in the 1990s.

Dr. Dale Van Steenis has been my friend and mentor as well as an important member of my family. We are closer than brothers. We have traveled the world together, done ministry together, fished in Alaska, Louisiana and parts unknown together and laughed together.

We have personally witnessed and heard stories first hand of God's power, stories that most of you would not believe unless you had been with us. Dale travels the world through his ministry Leadership Strategies training pastors and lay persons and helping poor people have a better life. Thanks for being there Doc and for believing in me.

Bob Walker has been my closest of friends and partner in crime and many other adventures for more than forty-five years. You have always believed in me and supported every crazy idea I've ever had. You've kept me out of more trouble than I want to think about. Everyone needs a friend like you Bob. Thanks for being there my friend.

Doyle Passmore has been my very close

friend and spiritual accountability partner for nearly two decades. Doyle, you've seem me through the good times and the bad, the times of blessing and the times of trial. We have traveled extensively together and have shared many great memories. We are brothers in Christ and friends for life. You have always encouraged me and stood by me when I needed someone who would tell me the truth. I can't tell you how much I appreciate your honesty, your encouragement and your loyalty.

In life we all have our heroes. My hero is a man named Ephraim Lindor. Ephraim heads up El Shaddi Ministries in Port Au Prince, Haiti, where he pastors a church of more than 400 people while working full time for Compassion International. Ephraim is one of the bravest and most generous men I have ever known. I can remember calling his number the Sunday morning in 2004 when President Aristide was being deposed. Ephraim answered the telephone and I could hear automatic weapons firing in the background. We have traveled together around Port Au Prince through some of the most dangerous places in the Western Hemisphere and he is always fearless. I have probably learned more about the value of humility and sacrifice from Ephraim than from any other person with the exception of Jesus Christ. Bless you my friend. You are an inspiration to me.

Dr. Tom Stout has been both my dear friend and my partner in ministry in Haiti.

Thanks Tom for your friendship and for your kindness and your unending generosity in our shared ministry in Port Au Prince.

Dr. Sean Growney is both my friend and my physician. Without your help Sean I would not have been able to do this project. Thanks Sean for your friendship, your skill and some great discussions about politics and the perils of universal health care.

Finally and most important I thank God my Father for the inspiration for this book and the strength to write it. I thank His Son, my Lord and Savior Jesus Christ for loving me when I was unlovable and for being willing to go to endure the horror of cross for even the sake of a single soul.

I am honored that you chose my book. I hope you find that you are both challenged and encouraged through the reading of this book. I pray for your success.

Bill van Steenis
February 15, 2009

✑ Prologue ✑

Don't Just Work for a Living

In 399 B.C. the Greek philosopher Socrates said, "The unexamined life is not worth living." He was being sentenced to death for persistently questioning the culture and values of his native Athens. He admitted that if they allowed him to live he would go on asking "Why?" and "How?" of anyone who claimed that they were wise and knew what was best in life. Socrates said that he had no choice, for "the unexamined life is not worth living."

Many of us *have* examined our lives. As teenagers we were certain that we knew everything. We also thought that we were special and invincible and misunderstood. Then, sometime in our twenties (for most of us), cracks appeared in our confidence. We still knew what we wanted but we began to realize that there were gaps, things we weren't so sure of. We realized that the world was a competitive place and that we might not be quite as special as we had thought: it turned out that a whole lot of other people wanted what we did as well. It dawned on us that if we weren't careful they might get it and we might not. That was frightening.

So lots of us tried harder. We bought houses, traded up. We made career moves, went all in with companies, partners and bosses. We made alliances in the workplace to advance our career. We invested in sure things like hedge funds and housing values. Some of us spent a lot of money and time on getting another degree at night or online. We went deeply into debt for educations and vacations and decorations (in our homes and on our bodies). It was all very expensive, but we weren't too worried because we were confident that our careers would pay off and our investments would pay out. After all, we were moving *forward,* toward What We Wanted.

As this is being written (in January 2009), many of us are finding that those cracks that started appearing in our twenties have become huge fissures. We don't know what we thought we knew. Even worse, we don't know what we don't know: we have blind spots that we can't check. The world economy may slip into a global depression. Many of our houses are worth less than they were ten years ago and we owe more than ever for them. Every day businesses are laying off thousands of workers, shutting down facilities, going into bankruptcy. Our personal, corporate and government debt is staggering, and the only solutions being proposed involve *more* debt: federal governments tossing *trillions* of freshly printed dollars and pounds and euros into bail-outs and subsidies and stimulus packages.

We don't know what will happen, but we are sure of one thing: all of this change is an opportunity to *re*-examine our lives. Many of us have been so busy working for a living that we haven't asked if we are working for a life *worth* living. Are we still sure that we know what we want? Are we still sure that we're special or invincible? Our teenage sense of uniqueness has proven false: we are not alone in what we are feeling. Many of us are losing a career, losing a house, losing a retirement dream--and we all feel pretty much the same way about those losses.

This is an important moment, a once in a generation opportunity to reexamine our lives. Not just our resumes, not just our careers, not just our mortgages or portfolios or budgets, but our *lives*. It's time to reexamine the nature of our work, our assumptions and values and skills and goals and ask whether our careers are resulting in a life worth living. Like Socrates 2,400 years ago, we can ask *why* we are working the way that we are and *how* we should live.

Let's clear up a potential misunderstanding right now: this is *NOT* a "stop and smell the roses" book. It's not going to try to convince you that there's a silver lining to losing your job because now you can spend more time with your kids and hobbies. That would be almost offensive in its superficial treatment of the devastating life experience that many of you are going through.

It's also NOT true that after reexamining their lives everyone will conclude that they should downsize or volunteer more, that they should adopt a slower pace or lower their ambitions. Let's be clear: we *hope and need* for some of you to conclude that your calling is to invent the next generation of technology, to lead the next Microsoft or General Electric, to make a fortune in the market, to leverage everything you have to go to medical school. Our country and world don't need *everyone* to be a teacher or a missionary or an artist. We need captains of industry, driven brain surgeons, venture capitalists who risk fortunes, skilled craftsmen who stay until the project is finished correctly, clerks who strive to become managers and managers who strive to make vice president. We need couples who save to build their dream house and ambitious investors who snap up bargains in real estate or stocks. The purpose of this book is to help you to go into the next chapter of your career content with your choices and with your eyes wide open.

The ReExamined Life is written for those of you who have not only lost a job but may be losing a career and consequently maybe a house, maybe a retirement.

It is written for those of you who are frightened, angry, grieving and anxious. It is about what to do next in your career and about doing it in the right ways, for the right reasons. Some of you may conclude that you have been working for the right things and go about finding a way to pick up where you left off. Some of you may decide that you have been settling for less than what you really want and commit yourselves to achieve *more* in your work or business. Some of you may conclude that you want a different career, one that is better aligned with your heart or values or circumstances. Whatever comes next in this reexamined life, you will not just be working for a living, but for a life *worth* living.

✤ Chapter 1 ✤

You Lost Your Job Today

Y ou lost your job today, and now all of your options seem bad.

Here's how it might have gone when you got to work this morning. Maybe you had been suspecting that today could be the day because rumors of downsizing or rightsizing or realignment or whatever "they" had been calling it had been in the air for weeks. The tension had been thick and the office chatter strained. There had been rumors and whispered guesses about who and why and when. More darkly, below the surface, there had been struggles and bargains and alliances as people scrambled to avoid being one of the victims.

Or maybe no one saw it coming. Other companies, other facilities or divisions or departments had been going through some turmoil, but your management had seemed positive and your numbers were solid. There might be some good, old-fashioned belt-tightening but at least you and your group were reliable and essential performers. *We'll be OK, ride this out,* you all thought. You figured that you were as secure as anyone could be in these times.

Maybe sometime before noon you were summoned to Human Resources. Maybe it was a call, or a manager came without warning and asked you to come with him. The walk felt sickening. You had to go to the bathroom, but you were following your boss and couldn't exactly ask to make a pit-stop, could you?

When you arrived they took you into an HR manager's office, or maybe into that little conference room where you once had your orientation and filled out your new employee paperwork. You would find it ironic if it wasn't so surreal. They asked you to take a seat and started talking. You didn't hear most of it because you got stuck on just a few sentences here and there: the company is having a downsizing and unfortunately your job has been eliminated. The manager kept talking (he or she was sorry) but your mind ran at full speed in all directions at once. It actually *did* run at full speed, as ancient human reflexes pumped adrenaline into your system and the fight-or-flight instincts written in your DNA churned in your lower brain stem. The manager kept talking and you tried to focus because they were explaining the severance and you really needed to hear that part, but like a page being repeated every thirty seconds over an intercom, you just kept hearing the news that you no longer had a job and there was no chance of being called back.

Eventually everyone stood and shook hands and said how sorry they were and good luck and all of that and then they escorted you back to your desk and watched you while you packed your stuff in a box and then they walked you out the door. Just like that. The whole sequence was one of the most humiliating things that you had ever been through. Everyone in your area tried not to watch your long march and the stripping from your cubicle of the family photos and souvenirs and awards, but you know that they did. They were terrified and helpless, like the seals on a rock when a great white shark plucks one of them. They were all wondering if they were going to be next.

You got to your car, put your box in the back seat, climbed in yourself and faced three awful questions: what are you going to do? What are you going to tell your family? And just how are you going to drive out of the parking lot with dignity?

Today you feel like you were set out on the curb like yesterday's trash. You feel worthless, hurt embarrassed and angry. You're also frightened and confused because there are practical questions, urgent questions, staring at you through the fog of anger and depression. You may have a spouse and children who are relying on you for their support, maybe their sole source of support.　What about the house payment(s), the car payment(s), the credit card payment(s)? How do you pay for your daughter's upcoming wedding or your son's equipment when football camp starts next month or the trip to your nephew's graduation?　Do you need to call your siblings and tell them that you can't chip in anymore for mom's nursing home bills?　Are your kids going to be crushed that Christmas will be lean or your spouse bitter that you can't go on that anniversary getaway?　You had already put a deposit down... can you get it back?　Why did you have to buy that new computer last month?

Now you have to find a new job. How are you ever going to do that in *this* economy? With so many people out of work, companies can afford to choose only the best, and you're going to look like damaged goods.　How do you put a good spin on this? Downsized, right-sized, realigned... in your mind you were *fired.*

●　　●　　●

You just got buckled into one of the worst emotional roller coasters that you'll ever ride. There are actual physiological changes happening in your body right now as all that adrenaline that rushed in today fades, leaving you exhausted and depressed.　Your appetite may have changed already: either you can't rouse the energy to eat or you're stuffing your face with comfort food. You feel worthless, but an hour later the anger comes back because you know that you *are* valuable and that you did more than anyone there and yet you were unappreciated. You feel as though you have failed yourself and your family, but an hour later you feel that the company management or politicians have betrayed you all. Being home in the middle of the afternoon feels weird and wrong, because you just left behind the people that you probably spent more waking hours with than your own kids. The place, the people, the company logo, the job title, the smells and noises and tools, the contacts, the projects, the purpose and the routine that used to give shape to your day are all gone. Like the victim of some terrible storm who emerges from a Red Cross shelter to find everything that they had ever called home has been blown away or flooded, you stand here with the clothes on your back and ask, "Now what?"

This kind of loss is, in the literal sense of the word, traumatic. The loss of a job or career creates psychological and physiological stresses similar to a death in the family or a divorce or the loss of a home. Tragically, sometimes the loss of a career can lead to the loss of other things. Depending on what you do now your marriage and home and health could be in danger.

You are going to be tested in every aspect of your life, in every dimension of your personality. You are going to learn things about yourself that you never knew. You may have to make some difficult decisions that are going to directly affect the lives of the people around you. It will test your relationships. It will reveal your character and the character of others. It will test your faith: your faith in God, in your country, in The System, in people. It will test your faith in yourself.

This will not be easy. This will not be quick. You will not have as much control – or at least the type of control – as you would like to have. At times you will feel helpless and hopeless, but you may discover help and hope that don't look like what you expected. The roller coaster will probably climb some hills only to go down again; but hey, that's what roller coasters do, right?

Yes, you lost your job today, and all of your options seem bad. Yet trust me enough to listen to one truth: it is possible – only possible, not guaranteed – that something good can come out of today.

It's a time for questions. Some you're already asking: *What happened? What's going to happen next? What am I supposed to do?* There are other questions, though. It will take time before you are ready to ask them, much less answer them, but they're out there: *What do I want? What do I need? What matters to me? What should matter to me?*

•   •   •

As I shared in the Prologue, in 399 B.C. the Greek philosopher Socrates had gotten in trouble with the ruling assembly of his native Athens for asking irritating questions about the city's culture and authority. Too many young people were starting to listen, wanting to hear the leaders give answers. They gave him an ultimatum instead: stop asking so many questions or face execution. Socrates said that he would have to accept the death sentence because it was impossible for him not to be curious. "The unexamined life is not worth living," he said.

You may have examined your life before, but after what happened today you are going to be forced to re-examine it. That brings possibilities, because in reexamining it you might discover things that you never knew or paid attention to before. That's what this book is about.

This book is not just about asking tough questions; it's about making tough decisions. There are seasons in life where you get to reflect without pressure and stress, but this isn't one of them: you need to get moving. You've seen movies where a group of survivors huddle around a crashed plane in a blizzard or bob in the ocean clinging to the bits and pieces of a sunken ship. In those scenes there is always one character who whines and wants to sit and wait for help. There's always some other character, usually the hero, who says something dramatic like, "If we stay here, we die." Well, this isn't just *like* one of those situations; this *is* one of those situations. You are now unemployed in the middle of one of the worst recessions, if not depressions, since World War II. You cannot sit around and wait for help from the government or

anyone else. You need to get moving, today, before the body of your former job is cold. You
need to reexamine your life in motion, along the
road. That means emotional multi-tasking. You
are going to have to work through the grief and
recovery cycle and the process of rediscovering
your identity at the same time that you are act-
ively and constructively dealing with your financial and other practical issues. The good news
is that this is not only possible, it's common.
Pioneers and soldiers and refugees have been
doing it for thousands of years. This book is
about how to do that.

This book is also about how to reinvent
your career. During my twenty-plus years as a
corporate head hunter I have learned some
simple truths about why companies hire people
and who gets hired. Despite the major shifts in
America's employment landscape, certain basic
truths remain (of course) basically true. Here's
one of them: the reason a company hires
someone is because they have a problem, so if
you want to get hired, be someone who can solve
that problem. Even better, be someone who can
solve *lots* of problems. Do not be someone who
whines about them, gets stuck on them or, even
worse, someone who *creates* them. At the moment, *you* have a problem, and it's a big one.
You're not the only one in this position today,
and lots of other people have been where you are
(both the guys writing this book have been there
more than once themselves). I want you to learn
to become a problem-solver, for yourself and for
others.

If you are already that kind of a person, great: your career *will* be reinvented and you will survive this. If not, I hope that this book will show you that it is possible, after losing your job, to discover a life that is more resilient, productive and joyful.

ஃ Chapter 2 ஃ

Eat the Frog

It's been said that if you eat a live frog first thing in the morning everything else that day will seem like an improvement. I don't recommend this as an actual technique for managing your day, but we can apply the principle: sometimes it's best to get unpleasant things, especially bad news, out of the way early so that you can move forward.

In this chapter we're going to "eat the frog" and talk about the worst that might happen to you now that you've lost your job. You are better off considering and coming to terms with the worst-case scenarios that so that your energy – and the rest of this book – can be invested in solutions. You cannot afford to have trauma follow trauma as your optimism and hopes are chipped away.

So let me say it: yes, those things that you fear most in this situation *might* come true. There may be no way out of this crisis except to go through some scary and heart-breaking experiences and to lose things that you cannot fathom losing. Before a doctor can get you to believe that a painful and expensive course of treatment is the best option for combating your disease, you have to hear and accept the diagnosis. You simply don't have the time to let denial and fear drive your decision-making or, even worse, shape your perceptions of the world.

You lost your job, but that could mean a lot of different things and we need to acknowledge that everyone's situation is unique. Let's consider the best-case scenarios first.

You may have just lost a job, not a career, and you may find another one fairly quickly. Perhaps there is a high and urgent demand for someone with your skills and experience within your industry and near where you live. If so, you will still go through a process of grief and loss, for all change is experienced that way, even changes for the better (graduations, marriages, births, etc.). You will also have to do the work of finding that new position and transitioning to it. You may be unemployed for a few weeks or a couple of months, but perhaps your savings or severance will cover that. If you're in this situation, be thankful. Keep reading, because this transition is a great time to reexamine your life.

In fact, *most* people are not in genuine crisis, even in early 2009 when this is being written. In the modern and developed countries of North America and Europe, even in the worst of times, most people have had a job and a home. During the Great Depression unemployment in the United States reached 25%: one out of four people were out of work. Not to be glib or minimize that pain, but the obvious truth is that even in the Great Depression three out of every four people did have a job. At the time of this writing the unemployment rate is running between 7-10% and climbing higher daily. That's a sobering and painful statistic, but the truth is that at the moment 90% of us are still working. Many of you reading this will find another job, and some of you will find one soon. Some of you will find jobs in your industry and this experience, while painful, won't be life-changing.

On the other hand, some of you are going to have a very difficult time finding any kind of work at all right now. There are all sorts of predictions about how long the current recession might last and how deep it might go. For this book to put any of those predictions into print today would be to set it up for failure when reality turns out to be something no one expected. Still, it seems safe to assume that the U.S. and global economies will continue to change and some industries will shrink, others will grow and new ones will be created. We aren't going to try and forecast which are which, but we do feel confident in saying that not all companies, careers or even industries will emerge from this recession intact.

That means that if you are in one of those industries your job may not be coming back at all. Worse, your *type* of job may not be coming back, or if it does, it might not return in the same geographic region.

Let me give you a specific example, literally close to home for me. For twenty years I have owned an executive search firm in Michigan, a state that has been badly hit by severe downturns in the automotive industry. My search firm has specialized in placing executives into the automotive industry, whether the Big Three manufacturers or their suppliers. During good times we placed highly skilled, highly experienced and highly educated leaders into high paying positions in highly profitable companies. But now, times are not so good in the automotive industry, and that means that times are bad in the entire state of Michigan, whose economy has been driven by this industry for a century.

For months I have been hearing from newly unemployed people who worked in the automotive industry. Shed your preconceptions about such people, because they have a wide range of skills and occupations. The automotive industry is made up of some of the largest and most complex companies in the world. I am talking to people who are graphic artists, computer software and hardware engineers, accountants, health care administrators, human resource managers, technical writers and engineers, designers and researchers of all types. They all played some role in this vast and complicated network of businesses thát resulted in new cars rolling off the lines in Detroit, and legions of them are seeing their jobs disappear.

They call me and I hear their pain but also their hope and optimism. They have great skills and have made great salaries. They have nice homes and kids in schools and sports leagues. They teach Sunday school or volunteer for local charities. They buy movie tickets, shop at the local mall, and go out to breakfast on Saturdays at the local pancake house. They have lives here, and they are essential to the lives of their communities. They want to believe that this lay-off is temporary, that I can find them another position, maybe with a competitor in town. They hope that they can polish up the old resume, change the route of their commute, and life will be able to go on much like it did before.

Except that I can't tell them that. The automotive industry is contracting, and whatever emerges from this season will be smaller than it is now. As it shrinks, so do the local economies that depended on it. Those movie theaters and malls and pancake houses and the people who work in them are starting to crack. Home prices are down and they can't take out another equity line of credit to see them through until their jobs come back.

This is where eating the live frog comes in: I'm having to tell these people, on a daily basis, that not only is their job not coming back but that there are no other jobs in the area to place them into, and there may not be for many months--if not years.   The bad news that they have to come to terms with is that they have not only lost their job and maybe a career, they may lose their house as well.

Their instincts and values are understandable: they want to stay in their homes, keep their kids in their schools, and stay close to their families and friends and churches.   But they are running out of money. The severance is gone, the savings is burned through, and they are drawing money out of an already shrunken 401k or IRA.

They need to face the bad news: they may need to leave their house and community and move somewhere else to find work, and that work may be different from what they've known and been good at. They may need to move from a four bedroom home in a nice neighborhood to an apartment and learn new skills, starting over at the bottom of another career.

That's frightening and heartbreaking.   It's what I meant when I said that some of you may need to do things that were unthinkable before now. How can you give up your home? That's where your kids learned to walk, where you opened Christmas presents and hid Easter eggs. Your grown children live in the area with your new grandchild. Maybe you share custody of younger kids, and leaving the area would mean jeopardizing your visitation rights. What about your parents? Your son was going to make varsity next season or your daughter is in line for a scholarship.

What would it mean to sell the house for

less than you owe on it? How can you do that? To give it up in foreclosure? After all these years, after all you have done or accomplished, are you supposed to just let it all go, move to another state and start life over again? There *must* be another way.

There may not be. What's happening in the automotive industry in Michigan is happening in other industries and communities across the country. People are coming to the slow and awful realization that we are less secure than we wanted to believe. The new normal is not a single career in life, followed by a retirement of endless recreation. People are discovering that they can't take for granted that their home values and retirement account balances will ride an ever-upward trajectory. They are discovering that they can't assume that they will be able to stay put where they are and not have to make moves, even late in life, to new places, new jobs, and new industries.

You may need to eat this frog yourself. You may need to accept that you will not find another job in your industry and in your area. You may need to accept that you will have to sell the house at the bottom of the market, maybe at a loss, or surrender it in foreclosure. That is not only heartbreaking, it can feel humiliating, another blow to the gut after the humiliation of losing your job and suffering though unemployment. You may feel like some sort of refugee, leaving your home to start a new, shrunken lifestyle somewhere else with less stuff, less prestige, less of everything that was comfortable and familiar.

It is important that you find a way to emotionally reconcile yourself to this possibility. I'm not saying that this *will* happen, but if you don't accept that it *might* happen, you will be blind to opportunities and dangers. Like the medical patient who doesn't fully acknowledge his condition, you will not be able to make wise decisions about your course of treatment.

•   •   •

For the record, you wouldn't be the first person in history who started over at mid-life or even later in life. In fact, millions, maybe billions, have done it before you: families who left prosperous businesses or farms in other countries because of war or famine or natural disaster to immigrate, often to America, to start over again.

My co-author went to high school in Orange County, California during the late 1970s. Near the end of that decade large numbers of refugees from the Vietnam War immigrated to the area. They came with nothing, living in small apartments or with several families sharing a small, rented house. They took entry level jobs. Greg remembers he and his high school friends hearing that the small, fifty-something man behind the counter at the convenience store or mopping the floors at the school had owned a bank or ran a factory or been a two-star general in Saigon. These previous members of the successful class came to a new place and did what they had to do. They started over, often late in life. Greg also remembers that after a couple of years their children became the valedictorians and got the scholarships, and the man behind the counter bought the store. They moved out of the small apartments and bought full-sized homes. They ate the live frog, moved past it, and built new lives.

The same story could be told over and over again about other countless immigrants from other lands, about Americans during the Depression or the Dust Bowl of the 1930s, about workers displaced when industries collapsed during other recessions.

Why would we believe that somehow we should be immune to what is a fairly regular occurrence in history, a normal if not common part of the human experience? These things happen. It's terrible when it happens to us, but what matters is not why, but how we will react to these adversities.

You've lost your job. What are you willing to do about it? Will you become a victim, waiting for someone else to rescue you? Will you become bitter because of loss? Are you willing to humble yourself enough to relocate, retrain and relearn to start a new job or a new career or a new life?

I am not asking you to go through anything that I haven't gone through or wouldn't go through myself. When my wife and I got married in 1983, I was fresh out of college and the entire state of Michigan was in what was pretty close to an economic depression. By the 1970s the whole nation suffered from double digit inflation, double digit unemployment and double digit interest rates. The big manufacturing cities of Michigan, which had driven the Industrial Revolution in this country, were falling into shambles.

My wife is from Cadillac, a small town in Northern Michigan, and I love it up there. I had a brand new accounting degree and lots of ambition, so we headed north to build a life among the forests and coastlines of the Great Lakes. I tried hard to find a job, I really did. I personally handed out more than 300 resumes and did not get a single interview. Unfortunately, there were simply no jobs for me in our little town. Neither of us had ever really lived away from family, and the thought of leaving everything we knew was intimidating, but we had to do something. I took a job in Texas and we left. I would be lying if I told you that it was a fun adventure. I didn't want to make this move and I fought against the idea with all my might. The bottom line was that there was work in Texas and there wasn't any in the Rust Belt, so in the end we made the only realistic choice that we could. We swallowed that live frog and moved on. It's not what we had hoped for but it's what life offered us. And in the end, it worked out.

You may have a similar story about when you were newly married and may be thinking, "Sure, but we're not in our twenties, we're in our fifties and we're too old to go through that again."

I can identify with that. As the automotive industry is drying up (again), my executive search firm (my career eventually led us back to Michigan and into this business) has suffered to the point where my wife and I are again, in our fifties, wondering if we should sell our home of seventeen years and start over again ourselves.

●   ●   ●

Consider this: lots of people remember those first years, when they were starting out and everything was an adventure, as the best years of their lives. They didn't hold onto things too tightly and their happiness wasn't completely dependent on their circumstances. Maybe, just maybe, for my wife and me and even for your family, this can be a time of new beginnings. No one would have wanted to go through this, but if you have to then you might as well go into it with the best attitude possible and find as much joy along the way as you can. After all, once you've eaten a live frog, everything else from that point on will seem like an improvement.

※ **Chapter 3** ↫

You Can't Stay Here

One of my favorite movies is *Saving Private Ryan.* The opening scene is a frighteningly realistic recreation of the Allied invasion on D-Day, June 6, 1944, from the point of view of an American soldier.

Landing craft called Higgins boats are loaded with soldiers approaching Omaha Beach in Normandy, France. As they come within range of the German artillery on the bluffs, shells start exploding all around them. Boats are being blown out of the water and soldiers are dying before they've even reached the beach. Men are scared. Some are praying; some are vomiting into their helmets. Finally, the landing craft ramp drops and immediately machine guns tear through the men packed tightly within. Some jump over the side of the landing craft, only to drown under the weight of all their equipment. The rest leap into the chest-deep water and wade to shore under withering fire.

The sand is cluttered with "hedgehogs": four-foot-tall steel I-beams welded into shapes that look like the "jacks" from a child's game. The Germans placed them there to prevent amphibious tanks from being able to drive onto the beach, but now they become slender shelters for some of the men to crouch behind. Machine-guns from the German bunkers on the bluffs are doing grisly work and everywhere there are wounded and dying American soldiers. The camera follows a man who has had his arm blown off. He wanders around on the beach looking for his arm, picks it up and stumbles forward in a daze. An Army chaplain prays over dying men. The sound of artillery shells exploding and bullets whizzing past is deafening, and the soft thuds they make as they catch a soldier is sickening. One by one the soldiers are cut down as they try to hide. They are paralyzed by fear: to leave even the thin cover of the hedgehog is to risk being cut in half, and to wade back into the cold Atlantic is to drown.

In the movie, as in real life, it was junior officers and NCO's (sergeants) who shouted an important truth at the men over the roar: *You can't stay here! If you stay here, you will die. You have to move forward, up that hill. The only way*

*out of this is to eliminate those bunkers and get
to the top of those bluffs!* One by one, in twos
and threes that morning, cold, wet, frightened
teenagers, raised in the hardships of the Great
Depression, gathered themselves together and
moved up the beach.

●   ●   ●

A lot of newly unemployed people are like
those soldiers. They see the carnage around
them and they cling to slender defenses: a
month or two of severance pay or a couple of
months' worth of unemployment benefits. They
are angry, depressed and frightened. Rather
than exploding shells and whizzing bullets, they
stare at the bills sitting unopened on the kitchen
counter, listening to the phone ring from collection agencies. The family has needs and there is-
n't enough money in the checking account to
cover them. They are consumed by fear. They
don't know what to do, but they hope that somehow, something will come along.

When the economy is running under full
steam and employers can't hire fast enough, a
month off while you regroup at home and send
out resumes might be survivable for most
people. That kind of passive job search is dangerous when the economy is in recession, unemployment is rising and some areas of the country
are saturated with highly skilled workers hungry
for jobs.

If you are sitting at home, paralyzed and

frightened like those soldiers on D-Day, let me be your sergeant and shout loudly enough to get your attention: *YOU CAN'T STAY HERE!*

That doesn't necessarily mean you can't stay where you are *geographically* (although as we said in the last chapter, you need to be open to the possibility that you can't). What I mean is that you cannot sit immobile, indulging your anger, hurt feelings or depression. If you sit here, stewing in negative emotions and hiding behind whatever savings or excuses you are using up, you will not survive. You will become even more of a casualty than you already are. The hit that you took need not be fatal or final, if you get up and get moving. Now.

•   •   •

So why *wouldn't* someone move forward after losing their job? It's common sense to note that someone who has only a limited amount of savings or severance or unemployment benefits and doesn't move quickly to find a new position, or who wastes time on unrealistic long shots or venting their spleen, is going to find themselves in deeper trouble fast. So what would keep someone stuck on the beach, unable to move forward or back? In my experience with newly unemployed people, there are at least three factors that sometimes keep them from putting the trauma aside enough to be able to take some action to secure their future: pride, emotional turmoil and indecision.

Paralyzed by Pride

Pride is a funny word. On the one hand we use it to describe a positive character trait: having enough honor and dignity and courage to work hard and face adversity. In fact, it is precisely pride that got some of those soldiers up and moving on Omaha Beach and that motivates some newly unemployed people to find new jobs or start new businesses. Yet pride has a darker side, and just as it can be a catalyst for action, it can incapacitate us during a personal crisis like unemployment. It can make you unwilling to consider all of your options and blind you to possibilities. It can drive you to deceive others, draw meaningless lines in the sand, hold personal grudges and take low-percentage shots, all in order to cling to a reputation (even if that reputation is largely in your own mind). I've known people who would leave the house every day and pretend that they were going to work to avoid anyone finding out that they had lost their job. I've known people who couldn't or wouldn't accept that the reason why they were let go is that they simply weren't as good at their job or as well-suited for their career as they believed that they were. I've known people who've lost a house to foreclosure after losing a job because their pride wouldn't allow them to sell it when they could have. I've known people who have lost a marriage after losing a job because their pride wouldn't let them move past their anger and sense of injustice.

Sometimes in life pride makes winners. Sometimes it causes tragedies and creates victims.

The opposite of this bad sort of pride is humility. Humility doesn't limit success; in fact, some of the world's most successful people have been quite humble. Humility isn't low expectations or acceptance of meager results. Consider Mother Theresa, a person of such great accomplishment and legacy that she is the only non-Hindu to ever be given a state funeral since India became an independent nation. She lived among the poor of Calcutta serving the sick and dying, often in their last hour. She was the epitome of humility, giving her life to serve other people and, ironically, it earned her a kind of spiritual authority. Far from being a humble wall-flower, Mother Theresa was a woman whose conviction was so strong that she scolded a sitting president of the United States for his position on abortion. She received the Nobel Peace Prize, but rather than keep even a dollar of the money for herself, she gave it all to helping those who have been left on the trash heap of society.

My friend George Beals is the Missions pastor at Central Wesleyan Church in Holland, Michigan, where I live. Several years ago George was traveling in India and happened to meet a Catholic priest who knew Mother Theresa and who asked George if he would like to see her work firsthand. Of course he wanted to, and so the two of them traveled to the Sisters of Charity offices in Calcutta, India. The priest asked

George to wait in a room for a moment. As he was waiting for the priest to return, Mother Theresa entered the room and introduced herself to George. George was awestruck by her presence. They had a brief chat about the Sisters of Charity work in India and what George was doing there as well. At the end of their conversation, my friend asked Mother Theresa how he could pray for her. Mother Theresa replied, "Pray that I don't get in God's way."

Her response is a stark contrast with what our culture values. Asked a similar question we might ask for prayers for things for ourselves, that God would grant our needs and wants and wishes, that God might bless our plans.

That's why pride can paralyze us after a job loss: it might blind us to the very real possibility that we might need more than a new job and might need to change more than employers. As a Christian, I believe that God meets us in our most desperate moments and works through them to change us for the better. Notice that I didn't say that God works to make all of our circumstances better, or that He always meets all of our "felt needs" or brings us immediate peace and happiness, but rather that He can use the most difficult things in our life to change us into better people and to do good, not only for us but for others. As the Christian author C.S. Lewis said, *"God whispers to us in our pleasures, speaks to us in our conscience, but shouts in our pains: It is His megaphone to rouse a deaf world."* Humility opens our senses, and our mind. Pride can close them.

Paralyzed by Emotional Turmoil

Tiger Woods once said that the reason that it is so hard to swing a golf club well is that there are so many moving parts in the golf swing: so many factors to the equation, so many different things that can go wrong. If so, then the golf swing is child's play next to the human mind.

We are complicated creatures, and our minds are complex things, with lots of layers and moving parts. On the physical level our thinking is affected by factors like sleep (or lack thereof), or diet (healthy and unhealthy), chemicals (foreign things like alcohol or drugs or the internal balances of compounds like adrenaline or dopamine or serotonin) and stimulation (light or noise or pain). We are a product of our upbringing and our self-image and our assumed and deliberately chosen values like pride and humility. We take in hundreds, thousands, maybe millions of inputs every day, and our conscious and subconscious minds make judgments and decisions about each of them. All of this activity, plus our choices and thoughts and a legion of untold and intangible bits of emotions add up to render our minds what they are.

Everything that I have ever heard about war and extreme survival incidents and various disasters has made the point that it is difficult to predict how people will react to stress. I started this chapter with a reference to the World War II movie *Saving Private Ryan,* and this unpredictability of people in stressful situations has become almost a cliché in war movies. Screen writers love setting up the muscle-bound, tough-talking guy to become a wimp under fire, or the mild-mannered English teacher (Tom Hanks' character in that movie) to become a rock of calm and leadership when really bad things start happening.

Over and over again, I have seen the confident executive or the rugged and worldly factory worker completely incapacitated by depression and indecision when they lose the job that gave them an identity and security. Even the strongest person can receive a mortal wound and ironically, the workers who have been the most successful, the most decisive, the greatest leaders inside the organization become paralyzed by emotional turmoil when they find themselves carried out to the curb of the building where they have given so much of their lives and derived so much of their identities.

All of the sudden the person who got up every morning and charged hard, who kicked rears and took names, who came home and talked shop, can't get dressed until 1 P.M. They surf the computer at home, supposedly looking for a job, but mostly reading news and blogs and watching YouTube (or porn). They talk endlessly about how they were unjustly terminated and the "case" that they are preparing. They cycle rapidly between anger and depression and manic fits of activity. They are going to do something, they are going to do nothing, they are sure things are going to turn around, they are certain things are going to get worse. They chase leads, but there are some things they can't bring themselves to do. They talk some more about how they were wronged and how stupid the company is. They rage at politicians on TV. They are going to write letters to the editors. They call former co-workers, craving gossip about what's going on at the company now. They don't return calls from co-workers.

Emotional turmoil has paralyzed them as surely as it did those cold, wet and scared teenagers behind the hedgehogs on Omaha Beach. Shell-shock, Post-Traumatic Stress syndrome, battle fatigue: whatever you call it, they have lost their ability to make and follow through on clear and rational decisions. They are becoming not only unemployed, they are becoming victims of the changes that life brings. Since the first woolly mammoth stepped on some hunter and on throughout the wars, famines, plagues, floods, fires, criminal rampages, invasions, persecutions, shipwrecks and economic downturns of history, millions--nay, *billions*--of people have suffered these types of stresses. Why do we think that losing our job is unique in the human experience? Yet throughout that vast reservoir of human pain, some people have been able to get up and move up the beach and some haven't. Those that did survived. Those that didn't are the victims of history.

Which will you be?

Paralyzed by Indecision

At the time I'm writing this, in January 2009, the news is buzzing about the "Hero of the Hudson," captain Chesley B. "Sully" Sullenberger. On January 15, 2009, US Airways flight 1549 (an Airbus A320) took off from New York's LaGuardia airport for a routine flight to Charlotte, North Carolina. As it climbed off the end of the runway a flock of Canada Geese flew right into its path. The flight crew heard and felt multiple loud thuds and their windows were covered with brown goose-matter. Passengers and flight attendants heard banging noises and saw through their windows flaming exhaust coming from the engines. At least two of the large birds had been sucked into the jet intakes, and 90 seconds into the flight Captain Sullenberger called the tower to report that he had lost power to both engines.

Sullenberger had only 3,000 feet or so of altitude to work with and very little time to act. Air traffic control told him to make a U-turn and land on another runway at LaGuardia, but he knew that he didn't have enough altitude and airspeed to execute that maneuver. Across the river in New Jersey, he could see the smaller airport in Teterboro but he quickly considered his situation and told the controllers that they couldn't land there, either. His mind rifled through all the data, evaluating every option as the plane lost altitude. He then calmly told the tower, "We're gonna be in the Hudson." He executed a turn, picked his target and adjusted his glide path. Commuters on the George Washington Bridge saw the A320 pass less than 900 feet over their heads. At the last moment he calmly instructed the passengers and crew to "brace for impact." He then controlled the aircraft down onto the icy river, bleeding speed gradually enough that the airframe didn't break apart. All 155 passengers and crew survived.

Sullenberger had spent his career as an Air Force fighter pilot, an instructor to military and commercial pilots, an accident investigator and consultant to the FAA on how to train other pilots to react in exactly this type of situation. He had spent thousands of hours in the air and in simulators practicing for something just like this. There could not have been a more qualified person flying the aircraft that day.

So was Captain Sullenberger some kind of fearless movie hero with ice water in his veins? Scientists who study such things tell us that the fear response in the human brain, centered in the amygdala, is automatic and can't be shut off. Sullenberger was probably just as afraid as everyone else on Flight 1549, but under stress he was able to think clearly, make good decisions and carry them out with self-control.

Pilots call this ability "deliberate calm." It is the practiced, developed ability to focus on the problem at hand in a crisis. Experience under stress can break some people, but others learn the ability to ignore the noise and chaos. They discover that when they remain calm, not only do they become more capable and confident, the people around them do as well. The same skills probably aid trauma surgeons, firefighters and other professionals who have to think and perform under great pressure.

The alternative is to pay attention to too many inputs, to be paralyzed by too much information and become stranded between too many options.

It's not too much of a stretch to say that losing your job can feel like losing both engines with too little speed and altitude to maneuver. Sullenberger had 3,000 feet: you might have three weeks or three months before you run out of money and make a pretty hard landing. You have to fight through the shock and surprise to identify your options (turn around? land in New Jersey? ditch in the river? can we clear that bridge?). This is a time for deliberate calm.

I have seen too many newly unemployed people unable to place themselves into that useful frame of mind. They become indecisive, cycling back and forth through all the alternatives, or flailing about, attempting them all at once.

Indulge me in another airplane analogy. In this one, the plane loses one engine over the middle of the ocean. The pilot comes over the PA and tells everyone they have to lighten the load in order to stay airborne. First you throw out everything that you don't believe necessary: extra equipment, blankets, books, water bottles-- that kind of thing. It's a start but it's not enough. The pilot tells you to continue lightening the load, but as you do the plane continues to lose altitude until you are in danger of crashing. Finally you toss out everything that you can tear loose: seats, luggage, even parachutes. After you have stripped the plane bare it slowly begins to gain altitude. You survived because you got rid of the things that were making the plane too heavy. But if you had hesitated and haggled and held onto too much for too long, it would have been too late. Again, it is the ability to be deliberately calm in making decisions and taking actions during a crisis that can be the key to survival.

Losing your job creates a financial crisis that is much like a plane that has lost an engine. You have to be willing to overcome your pride, take charge and get rid of the things that are wants rather than true needs. Getting rid of excess baggage may be the key to surviving long enough to reach your destination: full employment and restored financial security for you and your family.

•   •   •

After you've lost your job you can be paralyzed by pride, emotional turmoil and indecision. I am not trivializing the problems that you face or suggesting that the decisions that you have to make are easy. You may have every reason to be intimidated by them. The Germans on the bluffs over Omaha Beach weren't shooting blanks. They were real bullets and any one of them was capable of maiming or killing any soldier that left the cover of his "hedgehog." Yet – and this is important – it was precisely the gravity of the situation that demanded action. When the problem we face is what kind of takeout to order for the office lunch (Thai or Mexican today?), we can afford to hesitate and haggle and pout. When you are unemployed and facing the loss of your savings or your home or worse, you cannot afford to sit for too long, indecisive, emotionally conflicted, holding onto wounded pride. Others around you are moving forward and snatching whatever opportunities lie just up the beach.

❧ Chapter 4 ❧

What is a Life, Anyway?

A few years ago I saw a professional basketball coach being interviewed on TV about some camps that he ran for kids during the off-season. I can't remember who it was or any details, but one thing that he said has stuck with me. He remarked that when he asked the kids on the first day of camp what they wanted to be, they all said some version of, "I want to be an NBA superstar." The coach told the interviewer that it struck him that hardly any kids said, "I want to be a basketball player," or even something like "I want to play basketball when I grow up." They wanted to be stars. His point was that for those kids the love of the game took second place to dreams of fame and glory.

In one sense I don't think that the kids were completely out of line. After all, their parents had just spent what was probably a pretty good chunk of change to send them to a private basketball camp run by an NBA coach. Ambition is a good thing: without ambitious people society would stagnate, and in that context the kids' ambition and enthusiasm is understandable. Certainly Tiger Woods or LeBron James dreamed of being stars and breaking records at their age. Yet the deeper point that the coach made is valid: not only do we allow our career success to define us as people, we want to become successful *precisely so that people will* define us by our career. We want all the people who knew us when we were young to see us on TV someday (and be jealous if they were mean to us). We want to return to the class reunion and show off our trophy job, trophy car, trophy spouse. We want our parents to be proud of us for becoming captains of industry or brain surgeons or NBA stars... knowing that if we do manage to obtain those careers, mom and dad will, in fact, be proud of who we are because of what we do. It's often said that "we are what we eat." If that's true then it's even truer that, in our eyes and the eyes of many around us, we are what we do for a living.

Sometimes we have moments when, all of a sudden, our job seems irrelevant. Get a bunch of men together and they'll all squint at each other, trying to figure out what the other guy "does." But throw a bunch of dads together to

chaperone a field trip for their young children
and suddenly everyone's day job seems unim-
portant compared to their more important role:
this one is Trevor's dad, that one is Maggie's. Go
volunteer in a nursing home and try to explain
to the 90 year old woman that you're a "network
systems analyst." Good luck with that: she just
wants to know what's on the tray that you
brought or whether you can play the piano in
the lounge. Help to cook and serve breakfast at
a homeless shelter some morning and get anyone to care whether you're the "assistant regional manager" or the "assistant *to the* regional
manager." Look, can you make pancakes or not?

A few years ago my co-author Greg had one
of those moments that so many of us have had
when we ask where our job ends and our life begins. He was working for a large company that
was going through endless reorganizations, re-
criminations, purges and relaunches. When
Greg had started working at the company it was
a dream come true: he loved the nature of the
business and his role in it. As time went on, the
seemingly endless and meaningless changes
drained all the joy and sense of accomplishment
from his work. One day, staring out the window
of a plane on his way to another restructuring
meeting that would be full of pointless blame
and power grabs, he began thinking about all
the things in his life that he wanted to be known
for: relationships, volunteer work, creative and
useful things that he did personally and professionally. He pulled out a pen and began making
a list. *"These things are who I am,"* he thought,

"And whatever box my name gets stuck in on an organizational PowerPoint chart in this meeting is nothing more than my current job." By the time the plane landed he had determined that from that point on he would live and work in such a way that people would know and describe him by the things on that list and not by what was written in wet ink on his business card.

•   •   •

Here's the point of this chapter: *you've only lost your job, not your life, and your life is so much bigger and more valuable than any of the many jobs you will have during your lifetime.* The goal in reexamining your life is to figure out how to make your work contribute to a valuable life, not to spend the value of your life on work that gives nothing in exchange other than money.

Let me instantly head off three possible misunderstandings. First, there is nothing wrong with working to make money, even with the aim of making a lot of money, and there is especially nothing wrong with taking any work necessary to make enough money to feed and house and clothe your family. In fact, that is your *responsibility* and it has great dignity. Secondly, we are not to hold out against honest labor for an honest buck because we demand that our work be fun or that we find it rewarding or that it comes with sufficient status and perks and security and not too many hours or stress. Just so no one misunderstands, this isn't some pie-in-the-sky ideal about how we are entitled to work only on our terms. Work is necessary, it's often hard and it rarely earns us as much money as we want or need. It's often insecure.

But our work is not the same thing as our life. It can contribute to our life or it can corrode our life, leaving us scarred and weakened. A large part of our lives consists of work but we do not need to *waste* a very large part of our lives working. What's the difference? That depends on what we think that "life" and "work" are.

What is a life?

One of the most basic ways to define a life is as a measure of time. My life consists of the amount of time that my body and mind exist and function. One U.S. government publication listed the average American life expectancy as of 2008 to be between 77.5 and 80 years. Since there are 525,948 minutes in a year, that means that the average American's life would be about 41 million minutes of breathing and brain function. If we see a life this way, we are right to question the efficiency and value of how we spend each minute. Some things are terrible wastes of time, and while some things are enjoyable, some things actually give us a good return on our investment.

Of course we all know that life is more than just a measure of time. Many of us would correctly point out that it is also a set of experi-

ences that we have during that time. We figure
that some things that take a lot of time are
worth it because they result in a short but positive experience. Waiting an hour in line for a six
minute ride at a theme park might be a 10:1 ra-
tio of waiting to riding but we still might be
happy to make that trade. Some of the most
painful things in life, like an argument that des-
troys a relationship or act of abuse by a loved
one, might only last a few minutes but make a
life feel ruined. If we think about life this way
then we have to put all of our experiences in
some sort of cosmic scale to measure whether
the good experiences outweigh the bad and decide that we have had a "good" life.

We might think of life as a measure of results for ourselves or others. Did we accomplish
"enough" during those 41 million minutes to
judge our life to have been good or worthwhile or
valuable? Did we discover something (or did we
discover *enough*)? Save someone (or save
enough)? Impact people (or impact *enough*)?
Give something (or give *enough*) "back?" Leave
the world a better (or a better *enough*) place? If
so, then we might judge that the job we did added or subtracted from what we achieved with
our life.

Some of us talk of life as if it were the sum
total of a set of circumstances. We talk about
how hard or easy our life is or how much we love
or hate our life based on where we live, who
we're married to, the state of our health, the

nature of our job, how much freedom we have, the environment around us.   Most of us are kindhearted enough to feel grateful that we have a "better" life than that poor old woman we saw living in third world poverty or the mentally handicapped teenagers we saw getting off the Special Ed bus at the corner.

Some of us think of life as some sort of supernatural, animating force that is trapped, temporarily, in this body in this world. Many of the ancient Greek philosophers, some of them Socrates' pupils, considered a human being to be a "ghost in a machine": spirits trapped in a material world. A good life would be one that nurtures your inner being, allows you to be "in touch" with it, preparing you to eventually escape into the wild blue yonder. Seen from this perspective, a bad life is one that doesn't allow you to cultivate your inner life or focuses your being too closely on the trivialities of existence.

Contained in each of these perspectives is the notion that the difference between a good or bad life is something that can be measured, if not exactly quantified.   Either it has given us enough enjoyment, or we have done enough or we have enjoyed it enough. Therefore our work is either seen as a credit or debit to that account: we spent our time well enough (or not), we enjoyed it enough (or not), we did significant enough things (or not), we had a comfortable enough chair (or not), it brought out the beauty of the inner "us" (or not). We either value or re-

sent our work depending on how it is adding to
or subtracting from however we value our life.

All of those explanations are merely aspects
of life, but none of them is what a life *is,* essentially. Your life is more than a log of minutes or
activities, more than a balance sheet of experiences or accomplishments, more than a sum
total of your circumstances. You are not a ghost
in a machine.

You are a person, and your life is a story,
and both of those are eternal.

I am a Christian, and that is the perspective of my faith, but it's also the perspective of
many of the world's major religions. I won't
speak for them, but Christianity teaches me that
each of us has an identity, a personhood, and
that that personhood has a unique personality
and a consciousness. The Bible tells us that God
created mankind "in His image," with creativity
and sensitivity and memory and a will. When
our bodies die, our identity – our soul – is separ-
ated from our bodies, but we are eternal and
someday we will be reunited with our bodies in a
new heaven and new earth. Our lives have a
story, a long story, of all that happened in us
and to us and through us and around us. That
story will have good parts and bad parts, in the
ways that we've mentioned, but we are more
than just those elements.

This isn't a theological book, but consider
the benefits of this perspective. There is a terrible arrogance in all the other ways we use to
measure the value of a life: are you *sure* that

THE REEXAMINED LIFE   53

your life is *better* than the poor woman's in Haiti
or the handicapped kid's on the short bus because you can eat a whole bag of microwave
popcorn while you watch *American Idol* or because you can jog around the block with your
iPod? Do they have less dignity or worth, or
even happiness, because the circumstances that
you can observe, during this chapter of that
eternal life's story, seem less desirable to you
than your own? Jesus said (and this perspective
is consistent in all the world's great religions)
that God does not judge by the same standards
that we do. He considers other factors when He
eventually says, "Well done, good and faithful
servant."

It is tempting to judge the value of our life
in terms of what we gave, or "gave back," or the
"legacy" that we left behind. Again, who meas-
ures that? Against what standard? Did the
philanthropist who built a college library or the
businessman who leaves it all to become a missionary "accomplish" more than the faithful wife
who raised decent children and helped her hus-
band keep his business afloat? Did the lives of
the heart surgeon who saved thousands, or of
the activist who fed the homeless please God
more than the man who was kind to his sister,
kept his wedding vows and forgave and blessed
his father at his deathbed? The "butterfly effect"
is the notion that the flapping of a butterfly's
wings on the west coast of Africa creates a small
turbulence that, through an infinite and complex chain of events, results in a hurricane
slamming into Miami. In the story of an eternal

person, who is to say what the ultimate value of anything that we do will be?

Only one person can do that. There is a remarkable story in the Bible, in the Old Testament book of Samuel. God sends the elderly priest Samuel to the home a man named Jesse because Samuel knows that God has chosen one of Jesse's sons to become the king of Israel. Samuel sets eyes on the oldest son and thinks, *Clearly, this is the guy.* But God stops Samuel from giving him the job because God says, "The LORD does not look at the things man looks at. Man looks at the outward appearance, but the LORD looks at the heart." One by one the sons of Jesse are trotted out and one by one God tells Samuel he doesn't have the right one yet. In frustration Samuel asks Jesse whether he has any more sons. Jesse tells him that he does have one more son who is out tending the sheep, but surely it's a waste of time to bring him in because he's just a boy of no account. That boy's name was David.

Of course David eventually became king, and while he does some great things, he also does some pretty rotten things as well. He murders a neighbor to cover up his adultery with the man's wife. He was pretty much a total disaster as a father: his eldest son rapes his daughter; his third son kills the first son and leads a coup against David to steal the kingdom. And yet God calls David "a man after my own heart." Why? Because God evaluates a life differently than we do.

You lost your job. This is merely a bad chapter in a story that will last for eternity... unless you let it become more than that. This doesn't affect who you are or the condition of your heart... unless you let it corrode your soul. You may be short on money, maybe for a long time. You may have to move into a smaller home, let go of some ambitions, live in a less expensive manner, take on work with less pay and prestige than before. None of that affects who you are or the value of your life.

In the New Testament the Apostle Paul explains that he has gotten to this point in his own heart. Of course Paul, like everyone else, would rather have a good meal than a bad one or a comfortable bed or shoes than a sore neck or aching feet. Yet none of those things can really affect how Paul feels about his life: *"I have learned to be content whatever the circumstances. I know what it is to be in need, and I know what it is to have plenty. I have learned the secret of being content in any and every situation, whether well fed or hungry, whether living in plenty or in want."* (Philippians 4:11-12)

What does it take to find or maintain that kind of an attitude in the wake of a job loss? It takes a conviction that your life is eternal and that this is only a small part of who you are, and that your life's story is very long indeed. It also takes a willingness to let go of things, not to hold on to too much, too tightly. Those of us who are parents roll our eyes at how seriously our teenagers can take things that we know are so temporary: the shifting allegiances of "best friends," the favorite songs, who asked who to the dance, the ups and downs of puppy love. We wish that our teens would pay more attention to things that, we have learned the hard way, really do matter over the long course of life. It doesn't take a lot of imagination to think that maybe God looks at how seriously we take the ups and downs of our careers, our homes or bank balances, and wishes that we would focus on the things that really will matter a trillion years from now, when life will just be getting started.

•   •   •

You have lost your job and that might mean that you lose some other things as well. But I'm pretty sure that your job loss will not cause many, or any, of you to lose as much as Horatio Spafford lost.

Spafford was a successful attorney in Chicago with a beautiful wife, a son and four lovely daughters. By any measure Spafford had a good life. In 1871 his son, Horatio, Jr., died of Yellow Fever, which would be enough grief for any man to bear. Yet while the family was still in mourning, at about 9 P.M. on October 8, 1871, a fire started in a small shed across town. No one knows how the fire started – a newspaper reporter later confessed that he had invented the story of Mrs. O'Leary's cow kicking over a lantern – but over the next couple of days the Great Chicago Fire leveled about four square miles of the city and killed hundreds of people. Spafford had invested almost everything that he had in Chicago real estate. On the heels of losing his son, Spafford was financially ruined by events out of his control.

Two years later the family was trying to recover. Spafford's friend, D.L. Moody, was going to be preaching in England and Spafford felt that joining Moody there might be a healthy break. He sent his wife and girls ahead while he wrapped up some business, with plans to join them there shortly. On November 21, 1873 their steamship, the *Ville du Havre,* was struck by an iron sailing vessel and sank into the icy North Atlantic. Two hundred twenty-six people lost their lives, including all of Spafford's daughters: Annie, Maggie, Bessie, and Tanetta. His wife Anne was picked up by a rescue ship. The loss of the *Ville du Havre* was an instant headline across America, but Spafford had no idea whether any of his family had survived. When Anne reached England she sent him a famous two-word telegram: *"Saved alone."*

Spafford, overcome with grief, hurried to England to reunite with Anne, but in the days before air travel that meant a sea journey across the same route that his family had taken. The journey gave him plenty of time to reflect and for his grief to give birth to whatever was in his soul.

As the ship passed over the spot where the *Ville du Havre* had sunk, Horatio Spafford took a pen and wrote what would become one of the most beloved hymns of the Christian faith, "It Is Well With My Soul."

When peace like a river, attendeth my way,
When sorrows like sea billows roll;
Whatever my lot,
Thou hast taught me to say,
It is well, it is well, with my soul.

Refrain:
It is well, with my soul,
It is well, with my soul,
It is well, it is well, with my soul.

Though Satan should buffet,
though trials should come,
Let this blest assurance control,
That Christ has regarded
my helpless estate,
And hath shed His own blood for my soul.

And Lord, haste the day when
my faith shall be sight,
The clouds be rolled back as a scroll;
The trump shall resound,
and the Lord shall descend,
Even so, it is well with my soul.

Spafford's story wasn't over. He and Anne went on to have three more children. One of them, a son, died in infancy. In 1881 he and Anne and the children moved to Jerusalem, where they spent the rest of their lives helping to found a mission to the poor.

•   •   •

We started this chapter by talking about
the kids at basketball camp who don't just want
to play the game, they want to play the game for
the money and status it brings. It's almost a
cliché to point out that any of those kids, even
the most talented, could have a basketball career ruined by an injury, leaving them with no
prize, no point to their journey. As I said earlier, the purpose of this chapter was to remind
you that you've only lost your job, not your life,
and that your life is much bigger and more valuable than any of the many jobs you will have
during it. As you reexamine your life, your goal
should be to figure out how to make whatever
work that you do contribute to making your life
– your personhood, your story, your heart –
more valuable and contented, not to spend the
precious stuff of life on work that offers you
nothing but money, and maybe makes you a less
contented, joyful and resilient person.

To make sense of that equation, we've spent
this chapter talking about what life is. It's time
now to ask what the nature of work should be,
could be, was supposed to be. We'll turn to that
in the next chapter.

❧ Chapter 5 ❧

The Problem with Dreams

It's one of the most inspiring scenes in movie history. Rocky Balboa, the "Italian Stallion," rises before dawn in his cheap apartment. His workout clothes are dirty and threadbare. He yawns, half asleep, cracking raw eggs into a glass. The audience winces as he downs the entire mess, yolks bobbing and egg white dripping down his chin. He wipes his mouth on his sleeve, stumbles into the darkened street and slowly jogs away through the rough neighborhood.

Over the course of the movie Rocky gets in shape for the big title fight, and his morning runs get faster as he dodges early morning delivery trucks and sprints along the waterfront. No one who has seen it will ever forget the scene of Rocky, finally in fighting form, charging up the steps of the Philadelphia Museum of Art, pumping his arms in triumph.

Americans of my generation can't hear the Rocky theme song without our hearts beating faster and without believing that we can do or be anything that we want if we will only believe in dreams and work hard enough at them.

Now consider another scene, this one from television history. It's in the lobby of a convention center where hundreds of contestants are waiting for their turn to make their dreams a reality. The host of the show, Ryan Seacrest, interviews a young man or woman about their ambitions. They are supremely self-confident. They tell Seacrest that music is their life, that they have prepared for this moment as hard as Rocky trained for that fight. They tell him that, yes, they *will* be the next "American Idol." Some even go so far as to say that it's really not fair to the other contestants having to go up against someone like them, who is just about already a professional singer. In fact, they are the total package of an entertainer, the proverbial "triple threat" who can sing, dance *and* act (and wrote their own music and designed their own costume as well!).

You know what happens next. The poor, self-deluded soul becomes a national laughing-stock as they enter the audition room, where they are put on the spot, forced to drop the posing and dancing and other showmanship and told to just simply carry a tune, on key, for a few seconds without accompaniment. That's when they get hit with the human 2x4 of reality and truth-telling that *is* Simon Cowell. It's painful to watch, but often the person who has just humili- ated themselves in front of millions has a look of shock and denial on their face as the judges try to talk sense into them. Sometimes they argue and beg: the judges don't understand that they really, really *want* to be a singer, and if they were just given a chance, etc. After that, they walk back out into the lobby and some dig their hole deeper (the First Rule of Holes: if you're in one, stop digging) by telling Ryan that the judges didn't know what they were talking about, that they are still certain that they are an undiscovered star. Sometimes, at this point, we get a clue as to the source of the problem as their mother comes over and reinforces their fantasies, soothing their bruised ego by telling them that they *are* a great singer and not to listen to that Simon Cowell fellow. The camera shows them walking out of the building, mom probably on her way to buy them an ice cream.

●   ●   ●

Here's the problem with dreams, and the point of this chapter: our dreams can sometimes blind us to reality and cause us to miss real op- portunities while we chase fantasies. As a newly unemployed person reexamining your life and charting a course forward, you need someone or something to play the Simon Cowell role in your life, helping you to evaluate your options and sort out fact from fiction.

But what about Rocky? What about believing in a dream and making it come true? Isn't that what America is about? Aren't we supposed to think positively, believe in ourselves, create our own luck?

Some may snicker, but I think that Sylvester Stallone, who wrote *Rocky*, is not a bad writer and has more insight into life than that. We are so inspired by the craft of the film that we often don't pay attention to the actual story. Rocky didn't have a dream, concoct an ambition, work hard and chase opportunities trying to bring his dream to life. In the movie, Rocky has just about hit rock bottom: he loves to box – it's the only thing that he knows how to do, really – but he's not very good at it. His trainer tells him that he had potential but wasted it, had never worked hard enough. Now he's old, injured, and just about tossed out of the sport (the gym owner gives his locker away). He's all but an unemployed boxer.

And then he's *given* an opportunity, a million-to-one shot. When the top contender drops out of a fight previously scheduled in Rocky's hometown of Philadelphia, the current world champion and promoter of the event, Apollo Creed, decides that he could sell more tickets if he let a local fighter take the contender's place. Rocky is chosen not because of his grit, ability or because someone believes in him, but because of his *nickname*. Creed decides that fighting an Italian on the Fourth of July would be a great marketing ploy because Christopher Columbus, who discovered America, was Italian. So Rocky is chosen, basically out of the phone book, for his nickname, *The Italian Stallion.* Creed also picks him because it's a sure thing that he'll lose badly and quickly, making for a wonderful TV extravaganza.

In other words, it wasn't Rocky's idea to fight the world champion. In fact, it was a terrible misunderstanding, a bizarre twist of fate. And far from being an ambitious little dreamer, Rocky doesn't want to do it: his first reaction on being offered the fight is to turn it down because "it wouldn't be right": he had no business going in the ring with the world's best fighter. He doesn't want the humiliation of getting beaten up in the first round on national television. As the movie progresses, as he eats the raw eggs and runs up the steps, Rocky forms only one ambition: to not embarrass himself, to have the dignity to "go the distance" by not getting knocked out.

Rocky is really the story of an unemployed boxer who takes an almost accidental chance that fate delivers and does his best to not screw it up. It is not a template for every wannabe with more ambition than ability, convinced that life is holding them back.

What's even more poignant is that, in the film, Rocky *does* form one dream and pursue it relentlessly against odds and resistance, but it's not a dream to become the heavyweight champion of the world. He sees an introverted and withdrawn girl who works in the neighborhood pet shop and dreams of her becoming his wife. In a sense it's hard to say what the film is really about, because his training for the big fight is woven into the story of him wooing her, and he values her more than he does winning the match. We all remember him running up the steps, but we also remember that the first thing that he did when the fight was over, *before he had found out whether he had won or lost* (even pushing away the officials trying to tell him the results), was to cry out, cut and bloody, from the ring, *"Adrian!"* She is what mattered most to him.

Opportunities or Ambitions?

We need to form and pursue ambitions and respond to opportunities, but we need to keep straight which is which. And as a newly unemployed person, under financial stress to re-launch some sort of career, you must be careful to not confuse the two.

The world would stagnate without ambition. Enough has been said about the power of dreams to motivate us and carry us through various obstacles that I don't need to say more. Insert here every pep talk or graduation speech that you've ever heard.

What's more interesting for our discussion are the limits of ambition. If ambition can sometimes carry us to great heights, it can also send us on wild goose chases, convince us to waste time or effort or resources and keep us from seeing other options. For every American Idol there are the poor, deluded souls who had no business auditioning or pursuing a musical career. For some, even the money spent on singing lessons could have been better invested.

Some of you are thinking: but what if singing brings someone joy? What if it makes their world a better place? Then by all means they should sing: in the shower, to their cat, in the church choir. And if learning to sing better makes them happy, then lessons are well worth it. I spend money on fly fishing lessons and I'll never earn a dollar from fishing (quite the opposite!), but I like the process and challenge of learning to do it better. It's fun and exercise in the outdoors and gets me away from my computer. Yet the people who told those wannabe Idols that they could become professional musicians – much less rock stars – did them no favors.

As you reexamine your life after losing a job, career or home, you need to be honest about your ambitions. I have seen many people, in frustration over a job loss, decide that it was time to dust off that dream that's been sitting on the back shelf since they were a teenager. So they spend their unemployment trying to write a novel or open a restaurant. I have seen desperate people go to motivational workshops or buy self-help tapes or sign up for multilevel marketing schemes because they became convinced that they could make BIG MONEY ($!) for very little effort if they just believed in their dreams strongly enough (and bought the workshops and memberships and materials). I have seen people spend their severance time applying for jobs that they had no realistic chance of getting based on their skills experience or the marketplace.

Should some people write novels or open restaurants or get small business training or apply for a dream job? Of course they should, just like some people should audition for *American Idol.* But they need to go into such ventures with a lot of self-awareness about why they are doing it and what their expectations are. This is an old paradox: there is always the story of some novelist who got 47 rejection letters before publishing a hit, and that keeps hope alive for everyone else. It's a logical fallacy wrapped in dishonesty: *all great novelists are misunderstood and got rejections + I'm getting rejections = I'm a great, misunderstood novelist.* If God has gifted you to write novels or cook or build furniture, then by all means do that. That doesn't mean that you're going to get published, open a successful restaurant or make a living running your own carpentry shop. Maybe you should go for it, maybe not. My plea is to be honest with yourself about who you are, what your real gifts are and what opportunities are available for you at this time.

Opportunity Knocks

That brings me to opportunities. They are, in a way, the opposite of ambitions. For the sake of this conversation, let's say that if ambitions are the supply side of life's economy, then opportunities are the demand side. Ambitions are what we want to give to, in some cases push upon, the world. Opportunities are what the world wants, or needs, from us.

Most of the successful people that I have met have an uncanny instinct for detecting and evaluating an opportunity. It's almost as if the wants and needs around them have a faint, green glow. They see gaps and shortcomings, the frustrations or unfilled expectations of people or businesses. Read a book on entrepreneurship and you realize that many of the greatest products and companies in history were conceived not because someone dreamed up an idea out of nowhere or accidentally spilled a beaker in a lab and discovered some new Wonder Thing, but because someone was trying to solve a problem. Often they went through countless possible solutions before they worked out just the right way to meet that need or fill that want. After that, ambition kicked in as they came up with a plan to sell that solution into the marketplace.

The same can be said for careers. Some people *do* form an early dream to grow up and be something, a doctor, for example, and work relentlessly at it. Some careers pretty much require an early ambition because the education and training is so long and selective and expensive, like doctors and fighter pilots. One doesn't stumble into being a brain surgeon at 42 years old by responding to an advertisement in the classifieds. Most of us discover and develop our careers as we go along through the opportunities that present themselves, often from unexpected sources.

As you figure out what to do next after losing your job you need to develop your sensitivity to three aspects of the opportunities that will present themselves: true vs. false, good vs. bad and faithful vs. unfaithful.

Is It a True Opportunity?

There are true opportunities and there all false ones, which are really not opportunities at all. People have always exploited the needs, hopes and fears of others by presenting "opportunities" which only benefit them. Sometimes this is a criminal act, and there are con artists who prey upon the newly unemployed with offers and promises that seem too good to be true. As a general rule, when something *seems* to be good to be true, it is. If there is even a chance that someone is trying to scam you, run away. Other times it's someone offering something of legitimate value, but it's up to you as the consumer to decide if that value is worth your time or money. There are workshops, job retraining programs and books for the newly unemployed (like this one, and I hope that you think that it has been worth the price so far).

You will hear of "job" opportunities that aren't really jobs: they are often sales programs that place all of the cost and risk upon you with the promise that, if you're successful, you can make a lot of money. Every now and then something like this works out for someone and their testimony is used by the people marketing this program to lure more people into it, but you should be suspicious of these claims. Sometimes they want money up front from you in some form (almost a sure sign that it's a scam), but often it costs you nothing. For the people offering this "opportunity" this is great deal: if I wanted to sell something, especially something intangible that doesn't require me to ship a product and takes no real expertise to sell, why wouldn't I want a vast army of people, all risking their time and money, spread across the land trying to peddle it? It costs me nothing, and if a couple of them get lucky enough to make a sale I'll send them a few percentage points of commission on the back end. Probably.

The best way to evaluate these "opportunities," unless they are an obvious scam (run away), is to ask someone who is knowledgeable about that industry for their evaluation. I had an unemployed friend approach me just the other day to ask my advice. They had been offered an opportunity to sell a product in an industry that I was very familiar with. After hearing about this "offer" I told them that the industry was saturated with that product at the moment and that prices and profits were being driven down, and that also that the next generation of products would hit soon, leaving anyone unfortunate enough to get into the game late (as the advice-seeker would have been) stranded high and dry, representing an obsolete item. Of course the company offering this commission-only position was eager to sign up representatives that cost them nothing in the hopes of squeaking out a few more dollars at the end of their product life-cycle. As desperate as this friend was for employment, I told them that they would only waste another couple of months that could have been spent looking for a real job.

There may be other, more personal opportunities presented that you need to sift through the True/False filter. A friend or relative might think that they have a great idea for a business and want you to go in on it with them; there might be a long-shot opening in a company across the country that will cost you $1,000 for a plane ticket to go for an interview, a degree or certification that you could go back to school to get (with student loans) in the hopes that it will qualify you for some position. There is no easy rule for evaluating whether these opportunities are real or not: each must be tested on a case-by-case basis. I strongly encourage you to seek out as many knowledgeable and mature people around you as possible to give you advice, then listen to them carefully.

Is It a Good Opportunity?

There are true opportunities that aren't good opportunities. That means that while they are real – there was a legitimate need, a legitimate solution, the people involved are trustworthy – the potential return on the investment isn't large enough to be worth the risk. In other words, there just isn't enough money to be made in the deal. A few weeks ago a friend of mine

was considering buying a local restaurant. The
current owner had been only breaking even for
the last few years, wanted out and was willing to
basically turn it over if my friend took over the
payments on the building and the costs. My
friend, who has an eye for opportunities, saw
that the restaurant wasn't achieving its potential: the hours it was open didn't track with the
clientele it was trying to serve, its menu could
be simplified and improved, the concept and
marketing could be tweaked. He figured that he
could take it over, let his wife run it, and they
could take it from a break-even operation to
running at least a small profit within a year.

As he laid it out, the key phrase that
jumped out at me was "small profit," particularly
the word "small." As I listened to his plan I was
counting the costs: even though it wouldn't take
a big sum of money to purchase it, he would be
tying up most of his cash flow and energy. His
current business would suffer. His wife would be
at the restaurant 12 hours a day, straining their
marriage. It would be a huge drain on this family. I had no doubt that this was a legitimate opportunity and that they had the brains and work
ethic to turn a "small profit" over the next year.
But as he walked through the numbers, it became clear that this wouldn't be worth it: there
were easier ways for this family to earn, or save,
that amount of money over the next year. Doing
the math, his wife would have been working for
about two dollars an hour and endangering the
well-being of the family. It was a profitable opportunity, but not profitable enough to be worth

it.

The same can be said for job opportunities that require relocation. I've already said several times in this book that you might have to relocate for work, but now let me give a caution about that. It's possible that relocation for a higher paying job somewhere else might cost more than staying where you are and taking something that pays less. You have to calculate the housing in the new area, taxes, commuting and other hidden lifestyle costs. You might make $10,000 more in a year and spend $15,000 to earn it. You might be better off staying where you were and adjusting your lifestyle to be more frugal.

It might be worth taking on those additional relocation costs if the new job involves the *opportunity* (that word again) to advance. Many of us have taken a new position because it opened doors to move up. Sometimes that worked out, sometimes it didn't. In my experience, someone trying to recruit you will never tell you that if you take the position you'll be stuck in it for ten years with no chance of moving up. They'll always dangle the possibility of a better job in the organization once you get inside. They may even believe it. But remember this: be careful, even if you're recruited by the CEO himself and he swears on his mother's grave that within a year he intends to move you into the slot that you *really* want as soon as possible, if you'll just come in and take this other position first. But all sorts of things can change once you take the job: the company's profitability, mergers and acquisitions, reorganizations. The CEO who made you promises could even get canned shortly after you get there and you could be seen as one of "his people" who needs to be purged. If you have an opportunity that isn't so good at face value (because of the position, the relocation costs, etc.) but has the *potential* to lead to bigger and better things... ask yourself first if it makes good sense to accept the position on its own merits. A bad opportunity that doesn't actually turn into a good opportunity later is just a bad opportunity.

Is It a Faithful Opportunity?

Suppose you have a true opportunity (it's not an illusion or a scam), and it's a good opportunity (you really will make enough money to be worth the cost). Why wouldn't you take that?

There is one other filter I'd like you to consider: is it faithful to your values? There are things in life that you could get paid a lot of money to do that would be obviously illegal or immoral, and I'm going to trust that you have enough sense not to seize those "opportunities." But what about the more complicated and subtle choices that we have to make when evaluating opportunities to feed our families, especially when our options are limited? What about the job that would have you spend so much time away from your family that it might endanger your relationship with them? What about the job that would have you selling a product that in

your heart you believe is wasteful or dishonest
or wrong? What about a job that subjects you to
emotional or verbal abuse? What about the job
that would place you in situations that might
tempt you in ways that you can't bear to be
tempted or compromise your moral reputation?
I'm not talking about criminal activities (run
away from those), but real situations in the
business world that we all have different toler-
ances for.

There are no simple answers and no universal rules for how to evaluate whether an opportunity will be faithful to your values in life. We
are all so unique, and the seasons and contexts
of our life are so fluid that something that is in-
tolerable for one person is bearable to another,
or even to the same person at a different point in
their lives. Consider time away from the family.
For years my friend Greg has spent a lot of time
traveling for his work. People around him would
ask how he and his family coped with that; they
couldn't fathom how that would affect their own
marriage or children or emotional life. Greg has
always answered that when his kids were very
small he travelled infrequently and his family
developed a lot of trust and intimacy. As the
kids got older and the travel became more frequent, his family found a sort of rhythm to it
and got used to his trips as being normal. They
adjusted other aspects of the family's life to
compensate. Greg tells people who ask that
when he sees soldiers in airports on their way to
an eight month(or longer) deployment, he feels
that he and his family can learn to adjust to him

being gone for eight days. The key has always been that he and his family love and value each other, and despite the adaptations that they have to make for his business, their commitment to each other is unchanging and non-negotiable. When you are faithful to what you value you can, like water flowing around an obstacle, find a way to adjust.

Another family might not survive that type of separation. I know too many people whose marriage couldn't take that heavy a travel schedule or whose children became strangers. Usually there were other issues, other conflicts in those relationships and the time away only exacerbated those differences. But that doesn't mean that the time away wasn't a contributing factor. Perhaps if they had chosen to be at home more, the relationship could have been preserved. It might have meant taking a lower paying job with less prestige and perks; it might have meant that the whole family had to downsize their lifestyle, but if they really valued the relationship more than the money or status, that would have been the faithful choice to make.

I once worked for a company that took advantage of its customers and suppliers. I'm a person who values professional relationships, a real networker, not just for the advantages they bring but because I really do care about people: knowing them, working with them, serving them. That's why I was so good at my job of signing up new clients for the company and building alliances with partner firms. The problem was that once the contract was signed the project would transition to other people in the company who would lie and manipulate to extract every possible cent of profit from it. The clients and partner firms felt abused and resentful. I reached a point where I couldn't take it anymore: I was well-paid but the hurt and angry looks that I got from clients and the hostility that I felt from colleagues at professional events wasn't worth what I was being paid. My opportunities in that company were real and profitable, but they were unfaithful to my values. I couldn't represent that company anymore and still be the person that I wanted to be in the industry.

As you evaluate the employment opportunities around you, please pause long enough to consider whether they will be faithful to what is most important to you. Obviously, what's important to an unemployed person is a job that keeps a roof overhead and food on their family's table. But when deciding between opportunities, ask yourself which one will most help you to become the person that you want to be. That may not always be the highest-paying job.

•   •   •

Rocky Balboa was a fighter. It was his essence, his being, his fundamental identity. For him, to live and breathe was to be a boxer, to be in and around the ring. He didn't scheme and over-reach, he didn't delude himself about his ability, boast about things that he couldn't do, dream dishonest dreams about himself, force his ambitions upon the people around him. He did take the opportunity that came his way and strove to become the person that he was meant to be, and in the end worked hard enough to ride his potential as far as it would take him.

Rocky really loved one thing more than boxing, and it's the only thing that he really set out to get: the shy pet shop girl with three sweaters and the floppy hat. Whatever twists of fate that came his way, whatever fortune he found in the ring, it was always for her and about being faithful to her.

In the first section of this book we talked about the pain of losing your job, and in this section we talked about how a reexamination of our life and work and dreams can give birth to a different--and better--way to live. My hope and prayer for you is that you will handle your ambitions and opportunities in such a way that you be true to who you are, work for what matters most to you, and be faithful in taking care of the good things that have been given to you.

∾ Chapter 6 ⍺

The Island

You've seen the premise over and over again in books, movies and television. The details vary, but whether it's *Robinson Crusoe, Gilligan's Island, Cast Away, Lost* or countless others, the set-up is always the same: an individual or small group is stranded on a deserted island with only a handful of junk left over from the plane or boat and forced to improvise in order to survive for an unknown amount of time, hoping for rescue. Since we can all picture the scene in our minds, let's trot this tired old plot out one more time and apply it to the newly unemployed person.

I want you to imagine your job loss as a plane crash or shipwreck, and that you're now

stranded on that proverbial desert island.
You're not alone, however: you're stranded with
your family. You don't know how long you will
be here (unemployed): it could be weeks or
months. Familiar as we all are with how this
scenario goes, let's imagine a series of critical
steps that you must take. This list isn't necessarily in sequential order; you may need to do
some of them simultaneously and shuffle the order of others. Some you may need to redo as
conditions change. Regardless, to move past
losing your job you will need to do all of them at
some point.

Step One: Inventory Everything That's Avail-able for You to Use

One of the first things that the survivors in
the movies do, after crawling up onto the beach,
is pillage the fuselage or shipwreck and search
the beach for any wreckage that washed ashore.
They also search the immediate area for anything that might be useful (coconut trees, la-
goons full of fish, items left by previous parties
on the island, etc.). They make a big pile, sort-
ing all the materials that are now available to
them and considering how to make use of
everything to survive as long and well as possible.

What do *you* have to survive your time on
Unemployment Island with? You need to make a
careful and creative inventory of everything that
you can use. That includes obvious financial resources and less obvious skills, relationships,

etc.

Start with your liquid assets. If you are a financially meticulous person who knows the current balance of every account, the amount and frequency of all of your bills, and keeps records, budgets and forecasts, then congratulations: you're ahead of the game. You probably already know just how far that you can stretch what you've got. Unfortunately, too many people have only vague ideas of these figures and can't easily or quickly pull the information together. I've talked to both men and women who really had no clue: their paycheck was direct deposited, their bills were all auto-debited and their spouse handled everything. They went to work, used the credit or debit card and as long as the cards didn't get declined or there were no phone calls from collections, then they figured that the amount going into the account must be more than the amount going out, so everything was OK. Some people would have to dig through junk drawers or boxes of old papers to find account numbers or don't know all the passwords to go online and check balances.

This as good a time as any to bring up a very difficult subject that is all too real and all too common: some couples cannot talk about money. I mean they really *cannot* talk about it. Their relationship is so complicated, conflicted or convoluted that any conversation about money leads to an ugly confrontation. People and animals naturally avoid painful things in their environment: they don't touch hot stoves, lean against electric fences or step into mine-fields. These couples have adapted by simply avoiding subjects that cause pain, conflict or even violence. They simply stopped talking about their money a long time ago. When they had good jobs, it worked: the direct deposits went in, the cards didn't get declined, they kept their mouths shut. If this describes your family, then this is going to be one of the most difficult aspects of your unemployment, and of this book, because this simply will not work here on Unemployment Island.

The subtitle of this book is "What is Possible After Job Loss?" What is *not* possible is that you continue to stumble along in blissful ignorance or in willful neglect of your financial details. This isn't a relationship book or a money management book, but please get one of those if you have to. I recommend anything by financial writer Dave Ramsey. Advice, however, isn't enough: you are going to have to find a way to engage with your spouse and family on this issue, to get an accurate inventory of your assets, debts, auto-payments, etc. Auto-debited bill paying is convenient if you have the money in the account and can plan and track it. But now that the paychecks aren't being auto-deposited you could find that some bills that you didn't even know about are wiping out your checking account when you weren't expecting it. You must know exactly what you have, what you owe, when you owe it, how it's paid, what can be cancelled or deferred, what your user names and passwords are and where your paperwork is. If you cannot or will not do that – and you and your spouse can't find some way to communicate and cooperate – you will *not* survive on this island.

So what financial resources do you have? How much in severance, savings, stocks, bonds, unemployment insurance? Any money in retirement accounts that could be considered, if necessary? Any gift certificates or frequent flier miles that can be used for expenses?

Do you have other, non-liquid assets which could be sold if necessary? Any valuable collections of stamps, ball cards, coins? We all love our toys, but if it's a choice between your house or your sports car, boat, motorcycle, guns, photography equipment or whatever else, then you need to put those items in the survival inventory.

You don't know how long that you're going to be stuck on this island. You need to buy as much time as possible for your job search. The more cash that you have available, the longer you will last. It's just that simple.

What else is in your inventory? Don't just think about your job search in your primary area of work history. What skills do you have that could be used for odd jobs to earn some cash on the island or turned into a side business? Can you do accounting, auto repair, painting, home repair, pool repair or maintenance? Can you build things, tutor, type, write or clean houses? Do you have medical training, home health care experience or an unused college degree that you could find a way to make money with today?

Add into your inventory any friends or family that you can stay with for a short time who live in locations where there is a healthy job market. That's a tool that you might need for survival. Just the other day I was talking to a friend whose business, which supported the automotive suppliers here in Michigan, collapsed. He couldn't afford to keep his house any longer, but his brother had recently gone through a divorce and was willing to let my friend and his wife move into his large, finished basement. He realized that his brother's offer was part of his survival inventory. He got rid of the house (at a loss), and he and his wife moved in with his brother and are now relaunching a new business from there. His brother's offer has extended his survivability window while he gets his new venture off the ground and seeks other work.

Put this in your inventory as well: do you have anyone who would be willing to be your mentor or coach? This whole experience may be new to you and it may require skills that you've never tried before. Maybe there is someone who can coach you on job searches, or how to start a business, or networking. Do you know someone who would help you sort out and organize your finances? Do you know anyone who has experience in the industries that you are searching in? Ask that person to meet regularly with you and hold you accountable for following through on advice and action items.

Step Two: Divide the Labor and Organize Work Parties

It's going take a lot of work to survive on this island. Coconuts need to be gathered, fish need to be caught, firewood chopped and the campfire maintained, the island needs to be explored, and on and on and on. This isn't a tropical vacation: all of this work needs to be divided and organized. Not everyone can get up and decide to gather coconuts today. If you're gathering the coconuts all day, someone else needs to mend the fish nets or whatever.

Finding a new job can be a full-time job in itself. Likely, you are going to have opportunities to do some part-time work: anything from odd jobs to helping out at a friend's business to starting your own part-time business from home. Plus, there's the value of spending some time volunteering (more about that in a later chapter). Your time will be as full while you're unemployed as it ever was when you were working, but your "normal" routine has gone out the window. The time spent networking and calling, driving to interviews, doing odd jobs or small business work will disrupt the family's patterns and can create stress and resentment. *Why can't you go run that errand or pick the kids up? You're not working, are you?* You have all these other things to do in order to keep a couple of bucks flowing and look for a new job. Tensions can rise.

You need to sit down with your family and figure out how you can work together to make it through this. You need to communicate and co-operate on what the job search will require: finding leads, making calls and going to interviews will take hours every day, and you need to approach it in a business-like manner (we'll talk about creating an environment suitable for that in a little bit). On the other hand, your spouse probably needs to take on some extra hours at their work. Roles and responsibilities may have to shift. Children or extended family may have to pitch in to take up the slack.

You might even want to enlist the family in the job search. Research is critical (we'll talk more about that later and in the next chapter), and maybe you have a spouse or older child that can help with researching job leads online. Perhaps if their computer skills are sharper than yours or their time is more conducive, they can type and print your letters and resumes. Do you have someone in your family who can help you organize and plan interview trips while you pick up some odd jobs or part-time work?

This is probably the best time to raise an idea that we'll talk more about later in the book: bartering communities. It's not a new idea; in fact, it's as old as the hills, but when we were all flush with cash, taking care of ourselves in a consumer culture, we never considered this sort of thing. You probably know other people who are also unemployed or underemployed. What if you and a few other families sat down and figured out how you could barter for goods and services during this period? Of course, we naturally did favors for each other from time to time, but I mean make a serious and organized plan to survive on this island together.

Does someone in this group know how to cut hair? Could they cut everyone in the group's hair, or at least the kids' hair, in exchange for other families driving their kids to school? Could someone change the oil in the other families' cars if other members of the group would bring meals over to them? Could someone mow a lawn in exchange for someone else fixing their computer so that they could continue their job search?

This is the sort of thing that people used to do all the time for each other in small communities, especially on the frontier. On a deserted island the survivors would have to cooperate and barter this way. It's actually a gracious and sustainable way to live at any time that brings us into deeper and more tangible relationships with each other. Perhaps one of the outcomes of this crisis will be that people may recover some of these ancient ways of living and working with the people around them, even after they find new jobs.

Step Three: Organize the Camp

I'm a beach person. Over the years I've

learned that everything becomes a total mess pretty quickly   in the sand.   It gets into everything, and the evening dew from the nearby water makes everything damp *and* sandy. If you drop anything it gets lost or nasty. The castaways in the movies always seem to figure this out because they build some really neat camps up off of the sand. My favorite was the giant tree house in the classic Disney film *The Swiss Family Robinson*. Everything was high, dry and organized.

Your environment is important during your unemployment. Most of us organized our homes for the pattern of our working lives. You may not have had a home office space because you didn't need it. Now you're trying to run an extensive and exhaustive job search from your kitchen table, trying to keep all of your leads and resumes and letters and financial papers organized in stacks and trying to use a family computer cluttered with the kids' games and spyware. You give your home phone number out to prospective employers and during the middle of a phone interview the call waiting keeps beeping with your daughter's friends wanting her to meet them at the mall. As you're trying to discuss a possible position with a prospective employer, the dog keeps barking and the kids are yelling downstairs. It doesn't create a professional image and it makes you feel desperate.

Your environment might not only be distracting from your job search, it might be depressing, as well. Your spouse and kids take off for work and school and you are stuck at home with the unpaid bills and the broken dishwasher that you can't afford to replace. The pressure of the situation gets to you and it affects your energy level, which in turn affects not only the effort you put into your search but the tone of your voice over the phone as you make your networking calls.

As you and your family divide the labor and organize efforts, make sure that you organize your environment and make it as conducive to your efforts as possible. I'm not advocating going out and spending a bunch of money on a home office or chasing your family away while you're working, but if you're creative there are things that you can do. It may mean that you do some of your search work from a relative's house who works during the day, or from the library. I knew a man who lost his job but had a friend that owned a business. The friend couldn't afford to hire him (and the business wasn't a match for his skills anyway) but the business owner did have an extra workspace that he allowed his friend to use for his job search. He could come in for a few hours a day, use a desk and phone and photocopier for resumes and such. It helped his friend keep a business-like attitude during his job search. Be inventive, but find or create an environment that helps you to be organized, efficient, focused and as upbeat as possible.

One quick thought about the telephone: if you can afford it, keep or get a dedicated cell phone for your job search and treat it as your primary business line. It will give you a consist-

ent number that you can put on cover letters
and resumes and be reached at. Keep it with
you at all times in case you get a call back. Set
up a professional sounding voice mail message
(*"Hello, you have reached... I'm not available at
the moment, but please leave a message and I'll
get back to you shortly."*). If you have phone interview, go somewhere quiet without distrac-
tions; sit in your car in the driveway, if necessary. That phone is your lifeline to the business
world during your job search. If you can't afford
it, find a way to adjust your finances and cover
the cost *without taking out a multi-year contract.*
Even better, get a pre-paid phone and see it as
an investment in your search.

Do I need to make the rather obvious point
that you should have a professional sounding
email? You may have a Gmail or Hotmail or Ya-
hoo email account, but this is not the time to
have a cute or funny handle: *partyanimal@-
something.com* or *sallysmom@something.com*
aren't going to create the right impression on the
top of your cover letter and resume. Open a new
one, just for your job search, that includes your
name (maybe with some numbers, like a zip code
or something after it) and stick with that.

Step Four: Plan the Work and then
Work Your Plan

After you know what you have to work with
and have divided the labor, it's time to make
some action plans. For argument's sake, let's
say that you determine that catching fish in the

lagoon requires setting fish traps and nets in the morning, spearing them at midday, collecting the catch in the afternoons and mending the nets and traps in the evening around the fire. If that's the fishing plan, then whomever has fishing duty needs to work that plan or there will be nothing but coconuts to eat.

Finding a new job will require a plan, especially in the current job market. You probably can't just make a few calls, post a few resumes on a job search site and then sit back and wait for the offers to roll in. Even in the best of times most of the jobs available aren't posted publicly: small businesses are especially prone to hire people that they know or hear about through word-of-mouth networking. We'll talk about networking and selling yourself later, but the point here is that you will need a plan for how to enlarge your networks, discover opportunities and react to them. You can't afford to take a haphazard approach.

Your plan might involve research, calling, sending resumes and making follow up calls via social networks, geographic areas or industry types. Whatever that plan is, be consistent, serious and business-like in carrying it out. This will be terribly difficult if you are distracted, depressed or disorganized, which is why all the steps in this chapter's "Island Survival Guide" are critical.

Your time can be an asset or a liability, depending on how you use it. You can fritter it away on low-percentage shots, procrastination and manic-depressive activity cycles. You can keep yourself on an even keel if you make a plan that says, "I will make X number of calls per day and send Y number of resumes, every morning from 8 A.M. to noon, then work my part-time job until 4 P.M., make my follow up calls at the end of the day and spend evenings sending email." Formulate that plan with your family, divide up tasks that can be divided, and then stick with it.

One critical aspect of that plan is good research on companies, postings, and industries. Spending the time to do good research will produce quality results. Garbage in means garbage out. Lightly skimming a few mega-job search sites and sending inquiries or making calls on a company without learning about what they do is not quality research. I have seen people go into an interview and try and sell themselves as the greatest thing since sliced bread without knowing what the company actually does or makes. Research can involve carefully reading websites, following links, calling other people that you know who might be familiar with that industry and a host of other techniques so that you can target your approach to an opening that they might have.

Follow-up is critical. You may call a company today, be told that they don't need someone, and then tomorrow they might lose someone whose position is a perfect fit for you. If you don't call back every couple of weeks you'll never know. Be creative in your approach: offer to give a few days of work for free as a sort of probationary trial or to work as a temp for a while as you continue your job search. What do you have to lose?

Make sure that your plan involves some routine of daily exercise and make that a non-negotiable. Walk the dog, jog, play basketball at the church or school gym, whatever it takes. Sitting around surfing job websites, sending out resumes, getting rejections or being put on hold will be stressful and depressing. Besides the negative health consequences, stress and depression can make you desperate. Please hear and heed this word of warning: *desperation is not attractive.* It comes through on the phone, even in emails, and especially in person. Even if your financial situation feels desperate, you cannot let yourself come off that way. Few things will impede your job search more.

One last thought about planning: build into your plan time to volunteer to help others. It will clear your head and stop you from feeling sorry for yourself. Self-pity is never a good character trait and it turns off prospective employers. Even a few hours of volunteer work every week can make you feel productive and energetic. Those qualities are evident in your voice and demeanor when you sit down for an interview.

Step Five: Explore the Island

In the movies the survivors scout their immediate area when they wash up onto the beach. You've now done that and inventoried your finances and other resources, got your family communicating and cooperating, built some barter relationships with a few friends to share expenses and came up with a plan for your day and search routine. Now it's time to make your world bigger by making the world around you a little smaller: it's time to explore and map this island.

You don't know what's out there. Springs of fresh water? Other sources of food? Ruins from previous inhabitants? Maybe other current inhabitants. There may even be some way off the island on the other side: an old boat perhaps, or maybe a research station that gets visited every few months and has a radio. The only way that you'll know is if you explore.

What I'm talking about is *networking,* the process of increasing your knowledge and web of relationships by getting to know what and who the people around you know. You know ten people, and each of them knows ten people. Within two degrees of separation (you know someone who knows someone) you theoretically have one hundred and ten people in your network (your ten friends and the ten friends that each of them has). If each of those people know ten others, then within three degrees of separation you theoretically have one thousand, one hundred and ten people in your network. In today's world, those people are probably spread across the country in many industries and types of businesses. If you could learn what all of them know about job opportunities and get them to pass those on to you, then the likelihood of you finding a job goes up exponentially.

This is what I mean about exploring the island: learning what opportunities exist (especially the majority of job openings and company needs that are not publicly posted) and getting access to them. The entire next chapter is devoted to networking and we'll cover the topic in detail there, but remember that this is a critical step in your island survival plan.

Step Six: Have a Contingency Plan

It happens at some point in every deserted island survival story: the castaways have gotten over the shock of the crash, figured out how to make it and reached some sort of equilibrium. Their camp is organized, they have a routine, they have enough to eat. And then "Something Bad" happens. Maybe wild animals rampage through the camp and eat their food cache, or they get attacked by hostiles that they didn't expect, or a hurricane blows their shelters away. Whichever the case, there is always the "morning after" scene as they survey the wreckage of their camp and realize that they've just about been set back to the point that they were at when they first made landfall.

You can't always avoid emergencies or having to make decisions during emergencies, but you can sometimes mitigate them by having contingency plans. Think through what you might do in various worst-case scenarios so that, should they occur, you're ready. This seems obvious but so few of us make the effort to do this sort of thing. On Unemployment Island the margins of survival are thinner than on the mainland and emergencies that are easy to cope with on the mainland can be devastating.

Have you thought through what you might do if the car breaks down before it actually does? What about housing options should your unemployment last so long that you can't keep the house? Relevant to your job search, what might you do if you need to get to an interview and you have a transportation problem? Maybe in your barter network there is a friend willing to be on-call to give you a ride or loan you a vehicle if you get an interview on short notice. If your computer crashes while you're waiting for an important email or when you've promised to send someone a resume, have you backed your files up onto a portable drive and do you know of another computer that you could borrow or use?

Step Seven: Watch Your Language

The words that we use and the tone that we use to say them are more significant than we realize. In survival situations, like on a deserted island, we can make our situation worse than it actually is by calling them by the wrong names or creating panic in others with our tone. In the movies, there is always the character who panics, shrieking, "We're all going to die!" They freak everyone else out and usually get slapped by the hero to calm them down, until they run out of the camp in fear and get written out of the story by being eaten, shot with a flaming arrow, falling off a cliff, etc. Please don't be *that* guy.

How do you describe your situation? Do

you use negative words? Do you describe every glass as half-empty, every setback as a crisis, every job that you didn't get as a disaster? I'm not advocating "happy talk" (I've been pretty honest in describing things in this book), but how you label things colors your reactions, and the reactions of those around you.

Remember that other people are watching and listening. The people you are calling and talking with can hear negativity and pessimism over the phone. You may think that you're telling them that you're a problem-solver, a go-getter, a high-performer and exactly the person that they've been looking for, but your choice of words and tone might be creating the opposite impression. This is true in written communication as well: you might think that your emails to prospects are honest and thorough, but are they actually negative and rambling? You might ask your mentor or someone with writing expertise that you're bartering with to read over them before you hit "send."

I cannot stress this next point strongly enough: *you must remain calm around your family and friends, especially your family!* Your spouse and children are watching. When you speak negative, critical or defeatist words, or allow your tone to convey anger, fear or depression, you destabilize your family. Small children, especially, don't understand sarcasm or exaggeration: after a tough day of job searching it isn't helpful to rant and rave about how you're all going to starve or be living in a cardboard box. Aside from the fear and pain that you create around you now, you are also modeling for your children how to handle stress in their lives. You must be honest without creating panic around you.

I said in the beginning of this book that this period would test your character and teach you about yourself. How you speak during this time is revealing. Freaking out, whining, blaming and throwing tantrums are immature and unhelpful. Your family will react by withdrawing or panicking themselves. You don't want them to do either, and they deserve positive leadership from you.

Step Eight: Find your "Wilson"

One of the better movies about someone forced to survive on a deserted island is the film *Castaway.* Tom Hanks plays a Fed Ex employee who is the sole survivor of the crash of a cargo plane over the Pacific. He washes up on the beach of a small island, and amid the wreckage that he gathers are a number of ordinary packages that were on the plane. One of them contains, of all things, a volleyball. Hanks, in a fit of whimsy, paints a face onto the volleyball and calls it "Wilson," after the name of the manufacturer stamped on it. During the years that he is trapped on the island, two of his greatest challenges are boredom and loneliness, and over time he begins talking to Wilson, just to break the silence and empty his soul. Wilson is his only friend on the island, his emotional center.

While you're stuck here on unemployment

island you need something to keep you emotionally centered, something that relieves your stress and refreshes your spirit. That will likely be something different for each of us. As a Christian, I like to think that in a similar situation I wouldn't talk to a volleyball but would pray to God, but who really knows how they will react until they are tested? The more important point is that you find something that keeps you mentally, emotionally, physically and spiritually healthy.

I strongly believe that physical exercise is critical. It doesn't have to be strenuous, but even going for a walk in a park gets you out of the house, away from the bills and the job search. It gets your blood flowing, wakes up your senses and relieves stress. Plan some exercise each day.

Beyond that, find something, or maybe a few things, that refresh you emotionally and spiritually. Read, attend a church group, join a club, talk to a friend, play with your children, chop wood, paint, play music, worship or meditate. Surviving on this island demands that you keep your wits about you, that you keep your energy level up and that you do not despair.

●　　●　　●

You *will* get off this island. When and how is not clear, but you will get off. Someday you will have another job, and after you do you'll look back and reflect on what helped you to survive and what mistakes you made. You will have changed, because an experience like this cannot and should not leave anyone unaffected. Every one of the steps that we listed in this chapter is useful, not only for when you are unemployed, but for when life gets back to "normal" as well. My hope is that your life won't ever get back to "normal," if normal didn't include living with the steps above. Having to learn these behaviors in order to survive might be a blessing if it causes you to live this way afterward. Manage your resources better, communicate and cooperate with your family, create a helpful environment, plan and use your time wisely. Be prepared, speak graciously and keep yourself healthy. Those things work not only on islands, but on the mainland of life as well.

❧ Chapter 7 ❧

Grow Your World

At noon today I was standing in line at the customer service counter of my local cable company. There were a half dozen folks in line, fidgeting and wondering if they could get this thing done and still get back to work before the end of their lunch hour. We all had either a copy of our bill or a dead cable box in our hands, there to complain about something, but directly in front of me was a thirty-something guy, dressed sharply in "business casual," whose hands were empty. When his turn came I could hear the lady behind the counter ask whether he was there to deal with a billing or service issue. He said he wasn't there for either, but instead would like to apply for a job with the company. The lady was nice to him, but not very helpful. She said that he needed to go the company's website, where there was a form for submitting an application. This cable company is a multi-state behemoth, and I suppose that it has probably received thousands, maybe tens of thousands, of job applications and resumes recently. As the job-seeker walked out of the lobby, I thought that he deserved points for the personal effort to go down to the company and try to speak to someone, but that his chances were slim to make any sort of human connection with this cable company in his job search.

Here are few basic truths about finding a job:

- Most people who get hired don't get hired by a company, they get hired by *a person within the company.*
- People who do the hiring *hire people that they like.*
- Your odds of getting hired go up dramatically if you can *connect effectively* with someone *early in the process.*

I think that the young man in front of me at the cable company today intuitively knew that these things were true, and so he did just what he should have done. He dressed neatly, went into the local office of a large, successful company and tried to meet someone so that he could make a human connection. He was hoping to impress some manager enough to stand out from the thousands of other people that would like to work there. The problem was that this large corporation had set up a system specifically designed to thwart his efforts. They don't want some local manager bringing in people that they know or some walk-in applicant that the he takes a liking to. The company wants to depersonalize the process, funneling all hiring through a huge, anonymous human resources system two states away from where we were.

That probably makes some sort of sense for the corporation, but I know from personal experience that even with that system lots of people get hired there because a manager knows or meets someone that impresses them and that they think can be an asset. The manager then lets Human Resources know that they have a candidate whom they would like to be considered and that individual is flagged through the process. The young man who walked into the lobby today looking for a job wasn't going about it the wrong way, he just didn't have the right connection or relationship within the company. His world was too small.

This chapter is about growing your world so that you will have more connections and relationships, spread out far and wide through a variety of companies. The success of your job search is directly proportional to how big your web of relationships is. I'm not making the tired old point that "it's not what you know but who you know," because it's actually both, with some other things thrown in as well. Even so, knowing people is the key to getting interviews, so the more people that you can know the more interviews you are likely to get. If your web of relationships grows—if you come to know more people in more companies in more places--your world effectively gets bigger, and your opportunities become more plentiful. Period. The process for making your world bigger this way is called networking.

What is Networking?

At one level, networking is relatively simple to understand, and technology has made it easier than ever to grasp and do. You know ten people, each of them knows ten people, and so on. Networking is connecting with people in exponentially expanding circles, so that the number of people that you "know" is vast. Social networking sites like Facebook, MySpace or Twitter make the mechanics of these connections relatively simple. You have a list of friends, and if you click on any of their faces on your page then you can see a list of their friends. You can invite those people on their friends list to join your friends list. Everybody can see a running list of one-line updates about what everyone is doing at the moment. I just checked my Twitter feed and discovered that a "friend" that I follow in England just got back from rehearsal and was having tea and toast while another "friend" in Texas is at their daughter's parent-teacher conference. I just let the world (everyone who subscribes to my feed and the feeds of my feed) know that I was drinking espresso at my desk and writing about how to network. You can also learn about all these people by reading their online profiles. I just discovered that someone I know in Colorado likes the band The Fray.

So Facebook and other sites have made networking easy, right? Not exactly. These relationships are superficial at best. I might learn what someone in San Diego's favorite ice cream flavor is or that someone in London moved into a new apartment. That isn't necessarily helpful to me in getting funding for my start-up business, selling copies of this book or finding a job. It's considered bad form to exploit these sites to sell or ask for favors. What makes networking so valuable for your career is not only the quantity (it is at least the quantity) but also the quality of your relationships, the extent to which you can develop professional connections that can translate into tangible opportunities. That being said, even large, relatively superficial networks can be a starting point from which to develop more serious professional relationships. For example, I can't exactly post, "I need a job" on Facebook and hope to get a lot of responses. However, my co-author Greg has a Facebook friend in England who is a playwright. Since Greg is currently working on another book that has some connections to the UK, he can send her a message asking if she can direct him to any good publishers the next time that he's in the UK. If he can get a name or an email address of an editor there—maybe even an introduction from his friend--he's a lot better off than he would be if he just walked into the publisher's lobby like the young man did at the cable company this morning. So social networking sites and organizations can grow your world if you use them wisely, with discretion, to make intelligent professional connections.

You can certainly use your networking opportunities unwisely, indiscreetly and to make silly professional connections. Later in this chapter we'll talk about the "Dark Side of Networking," which uses people and most often blows up in your face. In the next couple of chapters we'll also talk about the story that you tell about yourself. It's far too easy to alienate people in networking situations, making certain that they will never introduce you to their friends or do you favors. This afternoon, as I was writing and periodically checking my email and Facebook, I got another post from a friend of mine who exploits such forums to blatantly attempt to sell whatever money-making scheme he's into this month. Please, please, *please* listen to what I am about to tell you: there is an art to networking, to advancing professional connections, and that art is grounded in genuine respect for people, their time and their feelings. They do not want to click a link to your multi-level marketing website, they do not want to be trapped next to you at a dinner party while you repeatedly ask them to get you a job where they work, they do not want to have you ask them to buy your product or service every time that they see you at church or the gym. Networking is not seeing everyone around you as a "lead." There are books and tapes and workshops that will tell you that it is, and there are people that have made a lot of money treating the people around them like that. Trust me: such people are not genuinely well-liked and no one will return a favor for them.

One more thought about what networking is not. It is not a list of disinterested contacts that have no interest in hearing from you. For example, a number of years ago a friend of mine took a job running sales and marketing for a relatively small firm. During interviews leading up to the job, the CEO of the firm kept telling him that the firm had an extensive and high quality network of industry contacts across the country that would provide a foundation for taking the firm to the next level. On his first day he sat down in the CEO's office to begin reviewing these connections and making an action plan. What he discovered was that the firm had purchased lists of "leads" from one of the many marketing companies that provide such lists. The truth was that this was essentially direct mail or phone-book data: the marketing company had the name, business address and name of someone within hundreds of companies almost randomly spread across various states. In some cases the data was more than a year old. The CEO, who did not have good people skills and had alienated most of his actual clients over the course of his career, had taken to buying these lists and cold-calling companies to see if they would be interested in his products. My friend had expected to develop and leverage a professional network of former clients and partner firms. Instead he had to lead the marketing and sales people through what was essentially a direct mail and cold-calling plan, starting from scratch without any name recognition for the firm they were representing.

There is nothing wrong with cold-calling from lists of names or directories; in fact, we'll talk shortly about how to do just that. Yet there is an important difference between a network of human connections or referrals and cold-calling people that you have no relationship with. Cold calling can lead to sales and jobs, for sure, and you have to engage in it, especially in a tight job market. It may be the only way to get your foot in the door and make a connection. Yet it is always better, if possible, to grow your world by building relationships. Remember the truths I shared earlier:

- Most people who get hired don't get hired by a company, they get hired by *a person within the company*.
- People who do the hiring *hire people that they like.*
- Your odds of getting hired go up dramatically if you can *connect effectively* with someone *early in the process.*

Networking for a Job

Networking is valuable for all sorts of reasons, personally and professionally. If you have a passion for ice-fishing, totem pole carving or yodeling competitions, then you can find other people that share your passion and pass on information and tips. You can go to gatherings, subscribe to newsletters and get introduced to people all around the world like yourself. There's a real buzz in the group because you all want the same thing.

Networking for a job is fundamentally different than social networking. Not everyone in your network wants the same thing; in fact, lots of them want things that are mutually exclusive. It's what's known as a zero-sum game: if someone wins then someone else must lose. You want a job. Some employer has a job to give, but he doesn't care about giving it to you; he just wants to solve his problem, whatever it is, as quickly, efficiently and cheaply as possible. He wants to find the right person but he does not want to be pestered constantly by unqualified or unlikeable applicants. A lot of other people that you are networking with also want that same job. They aren't going to cooperate with you: after all, you aren't just fellow fans of some rock band, sharing stories and tips about upcoming concerts. You are competitors for a job which both of you need to feed your families. The person you are talking to may not want to introduce you to their best contacts because he may be working them for himself or on behalf of another friend or relative.

Networking for a job requires diplomacy, judgment and advice. You must think of it as an obstacle course: at every stage you have to pass some test to advance to the next stage. If you meet someone at a luncheon, at your kid's soccer game, on an airplane or whatever, you must convince them to let you pass to the next level. For example, maybe their brother-in-law owns a business and is right now thinking about firing an employee for some reason and is quietly searching for a replacement. Why would they pass that juicy tidbit about their brother-in-law's company to you? Stop and think about it for a moment. Would they tell you because you really need a job and they feel sorry for you? Perhaps. Because you're likable? Perhaps. Because they size you up and realize that you just might be someone who can solve their brother-in-law's problem? Perhaps. They will not make a connection on your behalf for no reason. They might know other people who need jobs as well. Every aspect of your interaction with them is contributing to their judgment about whether or not to give you their brother-in-law's phone number. You must be aware of this when you are networking for a job. You are always interviewing, with everyone that you chit-chat with at the school play, sit across from at the community pancake breakfast or make small talk with in the airport bar. You need to be conscious of "your story" and the impression that you make. Ask yourself whether you are successfully promoting those in your human interactions, however casual. I have seen chance encounters lead to interviews because a good impression was made. It led to the job seeker getting forwarded or recommended to an employer who was looking for a certain kind of person. This may look like luck, but as the old saying goes, luck is where preparation and opportunity meet: someone who can tell their story and make a positive impression whenever and wherever they need to is ready for any opportunity that comes their way.

A last thought about networking for a job: do you have a clear idea of what you bring to the table for a potential employer? Someone whose only message is that they are an out-of-work engineer who desperately needs a job is less likely to get a hot tip or be forwarded to another contact than someone who can articulate the problems that they can solve for a potential employer. Know your story, your accomplishments and how to present them, and be ready to do so at all times.

Vertical or Horizontal?

Here's a simple question without a simple answer: should you attempt to network outside your "vertical market?" For those not familiar with the term, a vertical market is a segment of similar goods, services or businesses which all serve the same general needs or purpose. Let's suppose that you were a quality engineer for an automotive supplier, say, a company that made dashboard instruments. Your vertical market might be defined as the automotive interiors industry. As you network for a new job, should you try to make connections only with other automotive interiors companies? Should you also be networking for connections in sales or education? The question is not quite as simple as it seems: while anyone would be tempted to chase any sort of work anywhere, you run the risk of making a negative impression. If you do strike up a conversation at a party and project the impression that you are desperate for any kind of work, regardless of whether you have experience or knowledge, you might get sympathy, but not many people will see you as the solution to their problem or a problem that they know some employer has.

You can horizontally network. If you see yourself as a quality engineer, or perhaps as a team leader, whose last position just happened to be in the automotive industry, you might promote yourself in networking conversations as someone who can solve both quality and people problems in a construction business or at a restaurant. The risk in horizontal networking of this type is that you could look so generic in your skill set that nothing about you stands out in particular. If you do invest time in horizontal networking by going to events, making calls, pursuing contacts, etc., then you need to ask yourself whether you are spending your time taking low-percentage shots. Is it possible that the former automotive engineer will get hired to coach girls' basketball at a private school? Yes. Is it likely? Not so much. Is it worth investing a lot of time in networking and chasing leads for that position? That's not for me to say (there are too many variables: was he a college basketball player? Is he an alumni?), but I feel that I need to point out that time spent chasing this might be better invested networking for a position that he is more obviously qualified for.

Remember the three truths that I've already shared twice in this chapter. For a third time, so that they will be burned into your retinas:

- Most people who get hired don't get hired by a company, they get hired by *a person within the company.*
- People who do the hiring *hire people that they like.*
- Your odds of getting hired go up dramatically if you can *connect effectively* with someone *early in the process.*

Vertically or horizontally, your goal is to make as many effective human connections as possible, as early as possible in the process of applying for a open position.

The Dark Side of Networking

I've already mentioned this, but it's important enough to elaborate on. The art of professional networking is grounded in genuine respect for people and sincerely valuing their time, privacy and feelings. I remember a number of years ago, during a previous recession, a particular multi-level marketing company recruited large numbers of people in the town that I lived in. In its training this company taught people to see every relationship or encounter as an opportunity to sell their products, or more specifically to make new recruits (their "downline"). My town was relatively small and it didn't take long until it seemed like I was hearing recruitment pitches all the time, everywhere I went. People who had never shown previous interest started joining Bible studies or coming to PTA meetings. They wanted to get to know me, meet for lunch some time. I began to cringe when I met new people who were overtly friendly. Pastors were forced to deal with recruiters who saw their church as an orchard of low hanging fruit and began to use church events to pass out business cards. Networking is abusive when it robs normal human interactions of their honesty, seeing people as merely leads.

Networking is also abusive when it lacks reciprocity. A few years ago I knew a business consultant who traveled quite a bit, working with organizations all around the country. He shared with me how many other business owners wanted to befriend him in hopes of getting a taste of his leads and contacts. Occasionally he would make an introduction or referral when he felt that one of his clients would be well-served by some other firm that he encountered. Yet he lamented that most of the time the person that he had shared a lead with never reciprocated and introduced him to any of their clients. They saw him as a source of leads, but didn't respect or value him enough to return the favor and help him find any new clients for his business. He told me that he often felt used, and well he should have, because people *were* using him.

I know that you need a new job, and need it badly. But if you slip over to the "dark side," if you start disrespecting and using people, if you abuse social situations and innocent relationships, it will backfire eventually. You might get away with it for a while, as long as you have a steady pipeline of new people to exploit, but those that you used will not trust you anymore. You'll quickly develop a bad reputation if you live in a small community or work in a small industry. As urgent as your situation is, and I know that it is urgent, simple decency and an instinct for self-preservation should keep you from slipping over to the dark side of networking.

Research and Cold Calling

The human connection is always best, but it's not always possible, especially during a big economic downturn with rising unemployment. You may not be able to grow your network wide enough and fast enough. That's why research is critical and cold calling is often necessary.

Planning your work is essential, but simply making calls from the phone book can be a waste of time. You need access to some industry reference guides. For example, when conducting searches for my clients in the manufacturing industry I use the Harris Industrial Guide. Your local library may have this resource. If not you can go to *www.harrisinfo.com*. These guides are not inexpensive and I suggest going to your local city or college library to find them. The Harris guides list every manufacturing company in the US with 100 or more employees. This resource generally describes what the company manufactures, what locations they have, the number of employees, and contact information for their headquarters, branches, divisions or plants. It will also list the decision makers and their positions at each location. This is the information you are after.

Once you have access to the company names, contact information and decision makers it's time to plan your work. You begin by considering companies you may wish to work for that are located closest to your home.

To maximize your success you need to plan each day. That means writing down sixty contacts for each day, because your job will be to make thirty completed calls before the day's end. You're probably wondering how you can complete thirty telephone calls in a day. It's not impossible; in fact, it's not even difficult. When my business partner Angela and I are networking for a candidate in our search business we frequently make as many as seventy calls per day. Let's assume that it takes three minutes to make a call (and that's estimating on the high side). Thirty three minute calls will take ninety minutes. It will have taken another ninety minutes to prepare your research. That's three hours each day.

I frequently talk with people who have been in a job search for several months. I ask them how many calls they are making a day and the answer is generally around ten. If they connect on every call and spend five minutes on the phone they will only have spent a total of 50 minutes that day making contacts. What are they doing for the other seven hours and ten minutes? Nothing that's going to get them any closer to their next job. This type of networking by cold call is critical to your success. It doesn't make a difference whether you are a CEO or a line worker, personal contacts and conversations are where more than 80% of all jobs come from. Only 20% come from recruiters and the Internet.

If you discipline yourself you can do this quickly. When I'm networking for a candidate I always keep in mind that I have the answer to some company's problem. I just have to call and find that company, because they don't know my candidate yet. The same holds true for you. You don't just have the answer to some company's problem, you are the answer. You just have to find them because they don't know you exist. Yet.

You are going to have some people who are nice to you, some who will hang up on you and some who will be rude. Just be polite and remember that they aren't rejecting you personally; they just don't have the specific problem that you can solve. Every time you make a call you are one call closer to an offer. Every day that you make your calls you are twenty calls closer to a job than all of those people who are only making 10 calls a day. You are also far closer than those people who won't make any calls and are sitting, waiting for their phone to ring.

As you call, keep in mind that you are not calling to ask if they have work. Companies don't exist to give you a job. They exist to make money by serving a need in the marketplace. The ONLY reason they will hire you is if you can solve their problem.

Network without Neglecting Those
Closest to You

Networking for a job when you're unemployed is an awful strain. Meeting people, making small talk, hoping to get a lead is an enormous emotional drain, especially when you feel a crushing pressure to find a job quickly. It's even harder if you're an introvert. In fact, cold calling can be actually terrifying for an introverted person, and when your self-esteem has already been battered by job loss, the seemingly endless calls without success can be horribly depressing. As I said earlier in the book, this isn't easy, but there is no way out except through it.

If you have a family, it's important to stay engaged with them during your search process, especially if you have children who are living at home.

Kids are often unhinged by an event like the one that you are going through. In fact, it's not just you who is going through it: you're going through it together. It's important to build time into your schedule to be with them in settings that aren't stressful. Your funds are limited but there are many things you can do together that don't require money. There are museums, parks, the YMCA gym, the Boys and Girls Clubs and many other options for family recreation. Look for coupons in the entertainment section of your local paper. Your children need to know that this has nothing to do with them and that everything is going to be fine. This is an investment in your family. If you have never invested much time in your family before then now is a great time to begin. A few hours a week of scheduled time with your kids can help them to feel secure.

•   •   •

Unless we are celebrities or professional sales people, most of us try to keep our world small and manageable. We can only afford to have so many friendships, get to know so many people, go to so many events. Most of us like to contain our world within the boundaries of what is comfortable and familiar. When times are good, this is a great way to live. But when we

need a job and live in a community with rising
unemployment, we need to grow our world, to
make it as big as possible.   That dramatically
increases our opportunities. Mastering the art of
professional networking is the key to growing
your world during this season of your life.

❧ Chapter 8 ❧

What Will You Do to Get a Job?

I have a friend named David from the nation of Malawi, in Africa. David came to the United States to attend university. He graduated at the top of his class with a double major in business and computer science while he worked three part-time jobs. David was very focused and for four years he did nothing but study and work. When David graduated from college he volunteered to work for a CPA firm for free to get experience so that he could become a CPA. During that time he also took classes to earn his MBA from Michigan State University with a double major in Finance and Computer Systems.

Once David had completed his degree he

went out into the job market. David worked as a temp for a well-known temporary accounting agency. The company sent David to an insurance company to work for a few days to fill in for someone who was out on vacation. While he was there the company had a major meltdown of their computerized accounting systems. As David was listening to the staff describing the problem he asked the systems manager if he could help. The manager didn't know what else to do so he shared the problem with David. It took the better part of the afternoon but David got the system back up and running. He also found the root cause and corrected it so that it wouldn't happen again.

The president of the insurance company came downstairs to meet David that afternoon. He asked David if he could do anything for him in return for his help. David politely but boldly asked the president for a job, which he got on the spot. David's career really got started because he was a problem solver when a company was in crisis. David went on to become the internal auditing manager for the insurance company. He was there about a year when he was offered the position of Vice President of Internal Audit for a bank. David's income went from $30,000 per year as a temp to more than $100,000 per year as an officer of the bank.

David learned the secret to having people pay you to work: solve a problem for them. This seems absurdly obvious, but for some reason many people—probably all of us at one time or another—forget it. Far too often we invert the formula and think that we should get hired because it solves our problems. At some level we think that we deserve a job because of our education or experience, because of our needs, because of our connections, because of our past service to the company, because of who we know or because we think that we are brilliant and it would be advantageous to the company to have someone of our genius on their payroll. To that list add another, more recent conviction: we deserve a job because we're an American citizen and our government and society should take care of us by providing an income. We may begrudgingly accept that we will have to do some work in order to get the paycheck and benefits, but in the end governments, companies and society at large exist to serve our needs, right? Isn't that the American Dream?

We are not completely unjustified in our notion that people get jobs for all of the above reasons. Some people do get hired for their resumes or pedigrees or connections or industry reputations. Certainly we have all seen ineffective people and wondered how and why they got their job. Nor are we crazy for thinking that America owes us a job, since many politicians keep telling us exactly that. All of those things might get you a job, and when the economy is booming they might even get you promoted.

But when times are hard, the hard truths rise to the surface. Companies and individuals hire people, as employees or contractors, who solve some problem for them. If you want to have work, solve somebody's problem.

What Problems?

The formula becomes a little more complicated when you ask what problem, exactly, does
someone need solved?   David, my friend who
solved the insurance company's system crash,
saw a tangible business challenge that was
causing anxiety at the highest levels of the firm
and fixed it on the spot. That's a dramatic but
simple example. Other problems can be more
subtle, and sometimes a person with what seems
to you like no real skills or accomplishments is
solving a problem for his boss that you just
don't understand. For example, I once knew an
analyst at a major company who was a marginal
performer, at best. He took little very little initi-
ative and, when he did, his ideas were often out
of touch or not constructive. When it came time
to give a major presentation to clients it was
usually lower level employees under or around
him that did the analysis and prepared the recommendations. These co-workers came to re-
sent him and couldn't fathom why the executive
vice president kept this guy in his position. In
fact, a few of them attempted to make end-runs
around him to the vice president, believing that
if they could show that it was they who had actually written the report or come up with the
solution, then they had a shot at being promoted
into the under-performer's job.

Their line of reasoning wasn't crazy: they
knew that they were solving the problems and if

only they could get credit for that, then it should have insured their future. But there was a piece to the puzzle that they failed to see, because the lackluster manager was solving a huge problem for the vice president. The company was based in the Midwest but often did business with part- ners and clients in New York City. The vice pres- ident was an accomplished person, but he was thoroughly Midwestern: he had gone to a state university, worked his way up through the ranks of small businesses in the Great Lakes region and liked snowmobiling, deer-hunting and back- yard barbeques. The lackluster manager, on the other hand, had graduated from one the most famous of the Ivy League business schools and been a star athlete there. Although he seemed to those under him to do very little, he did one important thing very well: he provided cover and credibility to the vice president in midtown Man- hattan. When his name was attached to a pro- ject, the partners in New York felt comfortable, when he walked into a presentation they listened to the analysis and recommendations, even if they were largely created by employees with less impressive credentials. He bridged a cultural gap for the vice president and kept important partners happy.

Those employees that didn't grasp the prob- lem that he was solving for the company became embittered. They understood that his Ivy League background accounted for his position, but they didn't quite get it. When they made end-runs around him to the vice president, arguing that it was actually their content that was impressing the people in Manhattan, they didn't realize that giving his job to them wouldn't solve any problems for the vice president, it would only create new problems. Yes, the junior analyst from a state college in Indiana was smart as a razor, but she simply wasn't going to keep the investors happy over lunch at the Russian Tea Room. Maybe that's not how the world is supposed to work, but it's the way that it does work. The junior analyst trying to upstage the Ivy Leaguer wasn't a problem-solver for the vice president, and that's why she never got anywhere in her battles with him.

Being a problem solver does not always mean being the smartest person in the room or even the hardest working. It means, especially in a business going through tough times, making more money for the company than you cost it. To carry it further, it means making more money for the company than any alternatives that they might have: if you become the most profitable solution then you are, by definition, valuable.

Don't forget that your cost is defined as not only your salary, benefits and operating budget, but the time it takes to manage you and the impact that you make on other people. I knew a brilliant engineering manager who turned out a great product and kept per-unit costs down and profits high, but he was considered "high-maintenance." He saw himself as a maverick, as the one person in the organization who would see what was wrong around him and tell the truth, calling out like a prophet in the wilderness.

Over time his bosses realized that whatever profit he was generating by engineering great products, he was costing them in time and anxiety, cleaning up after all the squabbles that he started. As times got more stressful at the company he was let go. He never really understood that he was costing the organization more than he made for it.

Remember that in very large organizations problems are localized. Solving a problem for the company as a whole or for another part of the company can carry less weight than solving a problem in your own department or for your own manager. I have seen managers protect one of their people during a period of layoffs because that employee solved some particular problem for that particular manager. I once knew a gifted executive who, for whatever reason, had never taken the time to master building complex spreadsheets with formulas and pivot tables. The company required executives to submit a lot of these sort of data spreadsheets, but she wasn't very good at it and didn't want to take the time to learn. One of her middle managers was not only very skilled at this type of work, she was also willing to spend time helping the executive prepare her weekly reports and often "brown-bagged" her lunch in a conference room with the executive, correcting formulas and fixing links before the reports went off to corporate headquarters. When budget cuts caused layoffs, guess which of her employees the executive went to bat for? She could shift work around in the department but she couldn't, or didn't want to, function without the person who spent lunch hours helping her prepare the weekly reports. The others who lost their jobs might have argued that they were valuable employees to the company, but they weren't as valuable to the executive.

The Smartest Person in the Room

In school we were rewarded for being knowledgeable, clever and articulate. In a labor union we're rewarded for how many years we have on the job. In a production facility we're rewarded for how fast and efficient we are. But the smartest person in the room isn't the one who knows the most about the product or one who knows everyone and everything that's happened in the company over the decades or even the one who has made employee of the month seven times over the last five years. The smartest person in the room is the one who figures out what the most relevant problem is for the group and then fixes it. That's the most valuable player.

How does that help you in your job search? More to the point, how do you get to show that you're the smartest person in the room if you can't even get into the room? How do you demonstrate that you're a problem solver when you don't know what a prospective employer's problems are yet?

You can research. Research takes a lot of different forms: in the last chapter we talked about using the Harris Industrial Guides to learn about manufacturing companies nation-

wide.   Company websites are also great resources, as are links to their corporate reports
or news articles about them. Take every opportunity to talk with personal contacts, mentors
and/or other people knowledgeable about a company or an industry in general. The more that
you can learn about the types of problems that a
company might have, the more that you can tail-
or your approach to a prospective employer to
present yourself as a problem solver.

For example, I have a friend who owns a
popular restaurant. After I had gone there on a
recent Friday night I commented to him that the
place seemed as busy as ever. His brow fur-
rowed with anxiety as he told me that although
the volume of people coming in, especially on
weekend nights, had been steady, their profitability had fallen dramatically. It seems that with
a tight economy families were still going out to
eat for birthdays, anniversaries, date nights and
the like, but that they were ordering smaller entrees (or sharing entrees), and not ordering ap-
petizers, drinks and desserts.   But they were
still sitting as long at the table as ever before,
which meant that the revenue per table was falling while all the overhead costs, including the
wait staff, remained the same.   In short, my
friend's restaurant was packed but barely breaking even.

Having learned that, I might assume that
other restaurants today are facing the same
challenges. If I were applying to be an assistant
manager of some other restaurant I might use
that knowledge and put a bit less emphasis on

some parts of my resume and talk a bit more about how I would address these problems. How might I help the restaurant increase the frequency of its table turns during a night? How could I help with "up selling" customers to order more, or more profitable, items? The point is to learn what you can about a business or an industry before you talk to them and find a way to present yourself as a solution to problems that they are likely to have. Be careful, though, that you don't come out as a know-it-all who would come in and start trying to make disruptive changes. That would make you a problem creator, not a problem solver. Let them see that you respect them, would work hard at whatever they need you to focus on, but that you are aware of some of their challenges and would contribute to solving them. There is an art to doing this well.

The second way that you can show that you are a problem solver is to highlight how you have solved problems in the past. Instead of stressing that you graduated from this school and worked in that company for umpteen years, point out the challenges that you have met over your career. Don't just say that you have an IT network administrator certificate, talk about how you led a department through a system migration and increased productivity.

The third way to show that you're a problem solver is more impressive, but also more difficult. If you find yourself in a situation where you can interact with someone from the management of the company that you would like to work for, whether that's in a formal interview or a chance conversation at the coffee shop, listen to them and be perceptive. Sometimes they will share concerns and frustrations about their business and—if you can think on your feet and have good people skills—you might be able to make helpful suggestions. Don't push too hard and come off as if you, an outsider, are telling them how to run their business. Whatever occurs to you has probably also occurred to them and they have probably tried it already. But if you can make some perceptive observations and have prudent insights into possible solutions, you have the chance to be seen as someone who can at least help solve their problems. You might come off as the smartest person in the room without actually being in the room yet.

Why a Degree Still Matters

If problem solving is the key to getting a job, then why worry about college degrees or certifications? If you can show your value to a manager or an organization what difference does it make where or even whether you went to college? There are two reasons why education still matters.

First, there are things that you learn at college that are valuable in the workplace. Take communication skills, for example. Employers assume that if you have a college degree that you either learned or demonstrated some written and verbal communication skills in order to graduate. In a technology-driven economy where business is conducted with partners, suppliers

and customers all around the world, communication skills are more important than ever.   The
ability to explain a problem or answer a question
in an email is critical in modern industries of
every type. At all levels of an organization there
are phone calls, conference calls, reports, inquiries, etc. How can a company make sure that
a new employee won't make a costly mistake in
an email, on the phone, in reading a report or
instructions from a supplier on another contin-
ent?   College may not guarantee good communication skills, but college graduates are more
likely to be able to read, write and speak effectively than those who don't have a degree.

Another reason why degrees and certifications matter to employers is that there are more
positions than ever before that require very specific skills, and the degree or certificate is evid-
ence that they have those skills. I have a friend
named John who works for a company that
builds industrial robots, the kind of machines
on factory assembly lines. When he was young
he started working for the company as a mech-
anic, servicing the robots. Over the years the
machines have become increasingly complicated,
especially in their control systems. They integ-
rate with software and computer networks, and
servicing them requires being able to work with
those elements. John has to be able to program
or correct their actions from a laptop, using several computer languages, and interface with IT
network administrators. As his industry was becoming more software-driven, John went back to
night school and got a two-year degree and sev-

eral other certifications. A prospective employer who has a problem with their robots won't know if John can solve their problems unless he can prove that he has these skills. That's what his degree and certifications do for him.

I had a friend from church call me a few weeks ago after I had completed a ReExamine Life Workshop. Bob wanted advice about where he could find a job. I asked Bob about his education and he told me that he had graduated high school and took a few college courses but that college wasn't for him. Bob is at a distinct disadvantage. There are simply fewer and fewer unskilled positions available these days. Because of advances in manufacturing techniques and the advent of robotics, many jobs have been replaced by machines or eliminated.

Bob will eventually find a job, but at what cost? He may to have to relocate and start over. This won't be easy because Bob is in his late 40s. He may have to move across the country and work for a lesser wage because he didn't take the time necessary to learn a specific skill that he can sell, a skill that will differentiate him from others who have no skills beyond being a laborer.

There is no shame in being a laborer, but when it comes time to make cuts, laborers are always the first to go. They are also the people who have the most difficult time finding new work at a living wage. If you are in this situation, regardless of how old you are, I encourage you to find a vocation that you can learn that will give additional value to your employer beyond being a laborer. I only say this because I don't want you to have to travel down this path again. I know how hard it can be. I've seen too many people go through this more than once in a lifetime. If you are a laborer, consider making yourself more marketable by getting some kind of specialized training.

•   •   •

What will you do to get a job? Will you get a degree, make hundreds of calls and send out dozens of resumes? Will you network relentlessly and be likable? Will you get a new suit, stand in lines, go to job fairs? If so, then good: you have increased your odds of finding a new position. Still, the most important thing that you can do, the "killer app" for job hunting, is to be the solution to someone's problem. Figure that out and you will always have work.

❧ Chapter 9 ❦

Telling Your Story

The *New York Times* called it "The Resume Mocked 'Round the World." *Forbes* magazine ran an article about it under the headline "How Not to Get a Job." The posh periodical *The New Yorker* called their piece "Aleksey the Great." When *The Today Show* did a segment, host Matt Lauer starred in a parody of it. It became one of those impossible to predict, lightning-in-a-bottle Internet tsunamis, spreading across YouTube and countless other websites and inspiring dozens of spoofs, some of which made their way onto network television.

Aleksey Vayner, a student at Yale University, made a video resume, or more precisely, a video about himself, to accompany his resume, and sent it to a Wall Street investment bank, hoping to stand out from the thousands of other submissions that such companies get. The thing is really indescribable: it has to be seen to be appreciated (it still lives on YouTube and all around the Web). In it Vayner talks about his philosophy for success, or more exactly the philosophy that had already led him to accomplish so much at such a tender age. As he rambles on, the video shows him engaging in what appear to be feats of amazing strength: bench pressing 400 pounds, serving a tennis ball at 140 miles per hour, executing suave ballroom dancing moves and karate-chopping a stack of bricks. Someone at the investment bank that got this video resume evidently felt that it was just too priceless not to be shared and forwarded it up and down the offices on Wall Street. It then exploded at web-speed across the world and the rest was history. Aleksey Vayner became a public figure, a laughingstock and a cautionary tale: *never, ever, under any circumstances* make a resume like this one.

You lost your job. We've talked about confronting the worst-case scenarios and adopting a healthy perspective on life and work. We've discussed what you need to do now and how to network for opportunities. Now we need to think through how you tell the story of your career, in your resume and in person, so that potential employers will see you as a problem solver.

Obviously you don't want to do it like Aleksey Vayner. His video resume, with the

proud title *Impossible is Nothing,* didn't give anyone at the investment bank that he sent it to the
impression that he would *solve* problems.   On
the contrary, watching it, one gets the impression that this guy would be a colossal problem.
In one of the hundreds of articles and web discussions about his resume, someone quipped
that anyone that pompous and self-deluded
would end up within twenty-five years as either
homeless or President of the United States. So
right out of the gate, let me give you the most
counter-intuitive tip that you will ever get: *you
aren't the point of your own resume.*

Your Resume Isn't *Really* About You

If you read the last chapter, then you can
probably guess what your resume *should* be
about: *the employer's problems* and how you are
the solution they've been looking for. Your resume is not about how you are the person that
they've been looking for their whole life (you
aren't). It is about how you are a solution, but
not a *generic* solution (a list of offices or shops
that you've worked in for the last twenty years).
You need to be a specific solution to a specific
problem that they have. Here's a hard fact: the
potential employer doesn't care about you: not
at all, not even a little bit. I guarantee that when
the employer is sifting through a pile of resumes, they have only one thing on their mind:
how are they going to get that job done, that
problem solved? *"The woman who did all the materials purchasing just left to have a baby: now*

who's going to deal with the suppliers? We're not going to last two weeks without someone getting on top of that situation!" They flip through resumes, spending less than ten seconds scanning each one, looking for a match, like you would rummage through your toolbox looking for the right screwdriver. They aren't looking at you as a whole person, they aren't contemplating the complex and wonderful drama that has been your life, they don't care about your high school swim meets or that you love to bake and paint watercolor landscapes. At that moment they want to find someone so that they can *use* them. The more specifically you appear to be a useful solution to their problem, the more likely that they'll want to interview you to learn more.

When you create your resume, you have to attempt a sort of out-of-body experience and try to see it through the prospective employer's eyes. You must tell the story of your career as it relates to them, not to your own self-esteem (healthy or fragile as that may be). Your resume is a marketing tool whose *only purpose* is to get you an interview. It is not your memoirs, your career file or that "permanent record" that "they" kept warning you about in high school. Think of it as a television commercial or a magazine ad that's supposed to stimulate a response in someone who sees it, and the desired response is to move your resume into the "Call Back for an Interview" pile on a hiring manager's desk. You need to intrigue and even tease the reader into wanting to know more about you. When it comes to resumes, less *is* more.

In over twenty years of working with thousands of job candidates and resumes, I have seen, time and time again, people who were terrible candidates (meaning they weren't really that qualified or wouldn't really be that well-suited for a position) get interviews because they had a well-crafted and well-presented resume. The inverse has also been true: I have watched countless candidates that were fantastically qualified and would have been terrific employees not get called in for an interview because they didn't sell themselves well on their resume. The shock to some of these folks is like the shock of a top ranked sports team that gets upset in the qualifying round of a tournament and never really gets to compete against the teams that everyone considered to be their true peers. It's heartbreaking to see really great people not get call backs to interviews because their resume was ineffective at communicating JUST how worthy they are.

How to Do it Right

Remember when you were in school and had to write a term paper or essay and some teacher had some really quirky and fastidious way that she wanted your paper formatted? The margins had to be exactly so much, or it needed to be in a certain font, or some complicated and nit-picky way that the bibliography or footnotes were supposed to be laid out? My co-author Greg remembers a high school creative writing teacher who gave him an "F" on an assignment to write a poem because he didn't capitalize the first letter of each line. Greg went to the library and brought the teacher three books by some of the most famous poets in history and flipped through pages, showing her that many of the greatest poems in history did not, in fact, have capitalized first lines. You can guess her response, which was the same response as your teachers probably gave you whenever you turned in something that wasn't formatted to their specifications: that's the way it's supposed to be because that's how the teacher wants it. They get to make the rules; you don't.

Let's be very clear about this: this is not about what I like or what you like, it is about what *the hiring manager* likes. I don't care if you adore some particular font, paper color, style for the margins, a certain type of bullets, or a really perky way to lay out your header text over each section. I don't care if your parents and friends all think that you're such a whiz with that desktop publishing software and how many compliments that you received on those invitations you made for the family reunion. I don't care if you have a degree in graphic design. Your opinion of how your resume looks is irrelevant. If you want interviews then the only thing that matters is what that stressed out hiring manager flipping through piles of self-expression thinks. Will they move it to the "Interview" pile or not? They get to make the rules.

To be fair, my opinions about resume composition and format don't matter either. Who cares what I like or don't like? My *observations,* however, should carry a lot of weight and you would be well-advised to follow my recommendations. Over the last two decades I have read thousands of resumes each year. By painful trial and error, I have observed which ones landed the candidate an interview and which ones didn't. I have made follow-up calls to hiring managers, checking on the status of a candidate, only to discover that their resume never got looked at seriously and was tossed aside. You might know more than I do about graphic design, desktop publishing and have a much more sophisticated sense of style. But I can tell you what hiring managers like and what will increase your chances of getting called back for an interview. At this point, would you rather have a unique personal style or a job?

If I sound a bit defensive on this point, it's because so many people won't listen when I tell them this. Far too often over the years I have given candidates a resume style guide, told them to follow it, and then gotten back from them something that bears no resemblance to what I asked for. When I asked them why I've gotten a range of excuses: *I didn't have time to do a more detailed job; I just used my old resume and added my latest job; my friend got a job recently and I used her resume format instead of yours; I couldn't figure out how not to use "I" or "me" in a sentence; I like to type in caps; I like brown paper; I like mauve paper; I like orange paper; I had more information than I could fit on two pages so I used a smaller font to fit it all in; I have always loved the way that that script font looks—it looks elegant, don't you think?*   The one I love most, though, is: *I like my resume format better than the format you provided.*   Again, at the risk of sounding arrogant: how many resumes have you successfully presented to companies during your career? I've presented thousands and field-tested the results.   Your success in this job search is going to depend heavily on how hard you work at it and how willing you are to accept advice from professionals who do this for a living.   No, my resume format isn't the *only* format that works, but it *has* worked for my candidates for more than twenty years.

In my workshops and in the companion workbook to *The ReExamined Life,* I have detailed instructions for composing a resume. This isn't really a "how to" chapter, but let me give you some general principles.

Make it the Right Length for You and the Position You are Applying For. It does not need to chronologically list everything that you have done since ninth grade.   It does not need to describe every function that you performed within every job that you ever had.   It does not need to describe your personal life or accomplishments, your marital status, race, religion or likes and dislikes.

That being said, let's talk about the obsession people have with the number of pages that a resume is supposed to be.   I hear about this all the time from people who read that a resume should never be more than two pages long. Remember that the hiring manager wants to get as much information about you as possible with as little effort as possible. A four page document with no employment dates and long paragraphs describing the complex details of everything that you ever did requires too much effort. Some people, in a bizarre response to having heard that a resume must never be longer than two pages, simply use a smaller font and shrink the margins, making it even harder for the hiring manager to use. Always think about it from the employer's point of view. Which would you rather receive: a well-written, attractively composed document in a 12-point font that runs three pages or a rambling, incoherent mess that's been squeezed onto two pages with an 8-point font and quarter-inch margins?

The issue isn't really about two pages versus three, or one versus two. The core issue is whether you have a concisely written document that provides the right amount of relevant information. If you're 23 years old, straight out of school perhaps, and applying for your first or second job, it's hard to see that you have enough content to go past one page. You may be a superstar: first in your class from Harvard University, you speak Chinese, did a internship with the CEO of Boeing and you wrote a novel when you were 18 years old. That's impressive, will definitely get you interviews, but it also will fit on a single page. On the other hand, perhaps you're a fifty-something executive who has held a series of positions in several industries over the years, has some specialized training and published a series of professional journal articles throughout your career. Three pages might be entirely appropriate to share the pertinent details. Unless you're running for President of the United States you don't need four pages for your resume (and even then you probably don't). Remember, less is more: you want them to bring you in for an interview to learn more.

Make Sure That It's Well-Written. A poorly written resume invalidates all the supposed accomplishments that you list. It *cannot* have misspelled words: not one, not *ever.* It cannot have poor or misused grammar, incorrect parts of speech or verb tenses that don't agree with the subject or object. If you don't know what those things are, get help in writing it from someone who does. In fact, even if you're a professional writer get someone to proofread it. I miss things in my manuscripts all the time. I always have someone, sometimes two people, proofread everything that I write before sending it to be published.

It is the content and quality of the writing that actually matters, especially in industries where resumes are being submitted electronically. Depending on the type of job, industry or employer you may not be asked to submit a hard copy of your resume. In fact, some companies or employment services won't accept a hard copy because they can't be easily stored and forwarded around the company. What they will probably want is a word-processing file, most likely in Microsoft Word or PDF format. In those cases the same guidance applies: create an attractive and professional document. Often a manager will have your resume forwarded to them as an email attachment from the Human Resources office and they may print it out so that it's easier to read or make notes on. You may see your document, with all its formatted glory or shame, sitting on a hiring manager's desk during an interview, printed on plain white copy paper, highlighted and underlined with her handwriting scribbled in the margins. So make sure the margins are big enough, the font not too small, and the writing crisp.

Some companies and employment services will ask you to enter your resume into an online form. Formatting won't matter at all since you'll be copying and pasting your content into boxes as plain text. One box might ask for education or employment history, another might ask for accomplishments or specialized skills. If you have no artistic touch for fonts and layout then you aren't penalized, but those who do cannot hide behind cosmetics. It comes down to content and writing quality, which must be excellent. Can I say it enough?

A well-written resume has specific characteristics that set it apart from all of the others on the manager's desk or in the computer system. It clearly and crisply defines your career; it is easy to read and glean information from. It is accomplishment oriented and value driven. It is to the point and easy to read. It is written in the third person, meaning that it doesn't use the words *"I," "me," "we," "they," "us,"* etc. It will use lots of verbs and very few adjectives. Its sentences will be declarative and written in the active voice. If you don't know what any of that means, get help. If you don't have the writing skills to put it together, find someone who does.

Accomplishments are What Matters

So what should the content of your resume be? As we've said over and over, what employers are looking for is someone who can solve their problems. The best predictor of future success is past success, so the best way to convince an employer that you will be a problem-solver is to demonstrate that you have solved problems in the past.

It's astounding how often people misunderstand this, believing that seniority or "experience" counts. I see resumes that proudly assert that the candidate has spent twenty-something years in a position. Big deal. In a booming economy or a seniority culture, maybe that counts for something, but all it tells a prospective employer in a tight economy is that you managed not to get fired for two decades. The employer wonders: *Is this someone that will solve my problem or someone that will plant their rear-end, not offend anyone and not break any major rules?* Again, big deal. *With the company struggling to turn a profit, will this person be a competitive advantage? Will they solve problems or blend into the wallpaper?*

Sometimes I see resumes that brag about "experience," measured as having visited lots of clients, attended a lot of industry conferences and having sat on numerous committees. So what? This is probably a candidate whose career has consisted of being an insider, a knowledgeable gadfly and part of the company's overhead. Once again, what reason would a hiring manager have to think that someone like this will be a problem-solver or a competitive advantage for his boss, his department or the company in general? In prosperous times, when companies are making money by the fistful, a company can afford people like this who grease wheels, give advice or sit in meetings that their boss doesn't want to attend. When organizations are throwing out everything but the kitchen sink, these kinds of employees are the first to go. And they often don't understand why, since they were so "experienced."

Your resume must stress accomplishments, and you need to review your career to understand and explain how in every position that you ever held you solved problems and brought advantages to your employer. Granted, some job types make it easier to quantify accomplishment: a salesperson can talk about meeting or exceeding quotas and a manufacturing manager can brag about having increased productivity. Yet if you think it through, in every position you can explain what you did as meeting a series of challenges. Were you an administrative assistant? Perhaps you could mention how you helped two managers and their staff achieve three major product launches in two years. Did you work in shipping? Perhaps you could explain how you found ways to maintain fulfillment levels through the consolidation of two facilities into one while transitioning to a new software track-ing system. Do you get the idea? Look at your previous experience not as time spent on the job but as meeting a series of challenges.

Even the education portion of your resume can and should be accomplishment, rather than experience, driven. Did you go to college for four years? Good for you. Did you do a senior pro-ject finding some new way to organize data or teach students using computers? That kind of problem solving might be good for an employer. Did you go to Brazil for a semester? That sounds like it was probably fun, but it won't get you a job. On the other hand, did you overcome language and cultural barriers while working with a team of other students to organize a clinic in a small Brazilian town on your internship? An employer might see you as someone who could help them organize a department made up of immigrant workers.

A word of warning about listing accom-plishments: never try to fake them. I have seen people list degrees or skills that they didn't have, make up positions that they didn't hold and list awards that they didn't win. I have seen people get caught in some real whoppers of a lie when an employer ran a background check. More companies are taking the time to investig-ate backgrounds and resume claims. If you have been dishonest by embellishing or omitting some fact—or by making up something that is com-pletely fictional--you run the risk of being ter-minated or having your offer revoked. It's better to get things out in the open up front, be honest

and live with the consequences. I have had candidates boast that they could speak French,
Spanish or German on their resume. Please understand: two semesters of college French ten
years ago where you learned to count to ten, the
major colors and a smattering of travel phrases
is not language proficiency. I have seen some of
these folks badly embarrassed when the interview begins and the interviewer begins to flu-
ently ask questions in the language claimed on
the resume. When the candidate didn't respond
in kind, the interview was over.

No matter what accomplishments and skills
that you list on your resume, they can all be un-
done by a phenomenon of modern life that might
be called "The Anti-Resume." In the earlier
chapter on networking I talked about the advantages—or at least what we can learn—from
social networking websites like Facebook or
MySpace. For too many people, particularly
young people, a Facebook or MySpace page has
completely undermined their resume. In fact,
they might not even realize that it's happening:
they just can't understand why they don't get
called for interviews. Yet in one recent survey almost a quarter of employers admitted (and
surely more just wouldn't admit) that they
search for applicants' personal websites. Once
something is out on the web, it's in the public
domain and there is nothing to prevent a hiring
manager from simply typing an applicant's name
into a search engine. If they find pages that in-
dicate that the candidate has a character, per-

sonality or lifestyle that contradicts the impression which they have created with their resume, then the odds of getting an interview fall quickly. While some might argue that an applicant's personal life should have no bearing on the employment process, the reality is that it *does*. Candidates who portray themselves as responsible, sober and respectful during the application process but have put material on the Internet that contradicts that impression should not be surprised when the employer chooses not to interview them. There is no reasonable expectation of privacy on the Internet, and all of us should think long and hard about our online "trail." Remember that major search engines store pages, so that even if you pull something down it will leave a sort of fossilized record which could haunt you for years to come.

I often get asked whether a person should have more than one resume, tailoring each to specific companies or positions, and I think that it's a bad idea. You do not want to have a bunch of slippery position descriptions in your resume, cleverly tweaking them to match the job you are applying for. What you want on your resume is clear record of your best accomplishments throughout a career which probably spans a number of different companies and job types. Your best accomplishments are simply your best accomplishments, the ones that most clearly demonstrate that you are an enthusiastic and hardworking problem solver. Employers are more interested in those qualities than that you had some similar sounding title in your last three jobs.

There is one exception to the one-resume rule: if you have the legitimate experience to work in two entirely different career categories and are applying for both. For example, consider a woman who has extensive education and experience as a software engineer, but in several of the smaller software companies she worked for she also had some sales duties. She might consider preparing two resumes, one for pursuing an engineering career and one for pursuing a sales career, each one emphasizing different accomplishments. This is especially true for older workers who are contemplating a change in career direction and want to explore the possibilities of a new industry or job type. In such cases, if they have sufficient accomplishments in more than one field, they might prepare a resume for each of the two career tracks.

What About The Bad Stuff?

Almost all of us have had setbacks in our careers, or even outright failures. Some of us didn't hit our numbers and got passed over for promotions or even fired. Some of us lost jobs because we weren't really suited for a job type, a position or a company. Some us didn't get along with a boss and lost our job over it. Some of us screwed up, made bad judgment calls and were terminated for cause over it.

Some of us may have done something even worse: we did something unethical, dishonest or abusive, got caught and it has haunted us ever since. I know someone who got caught embezzling from a company, was fired and prosecuted for it. She has tried to rebuild a career for years, but understandably employers won't put her in a position of any responsibility and she has worked a series of temporary labor jobs for years. How can she spin something like this on her resume so that she can get back into some sort of management position?

She can't, and neither should you. The first rule of resumes is to be honest, for two good reasons. First, because it's the right thing to do. I'm not going to even waste time explaining why dishonesty is wrong: if you don't get it, I can't explain it. Second, because the odds of getting caught in a lie keep growing with technology. There is so much information out there, and so many ways to gather it, that if you've got skeletons in your closet, you run a genuine risk of them falling out. As I'm writing this book in early 2009, the news is full of several high-level government appointees whose nominations have fallen apart because of problems in their pasts that were exposed during Senate confirmation hearings. You don't need to be a big-time politician for errors or omissions to be exposed. Don't think that confidentiality will protect you either, because if backchannel industry gossip torpedoes your resume, you'll never hear about it: you just won't get callbacks for interviews, and good luck trying to prove why, especially in a tight job market: when there are many more applicants than open positions, an employer doesn't need too much justification for selecting other candidates.

You are better off being honest, confronting your past, and working around it. In some cases you will be able to overcome it: if you can solve a problem that a manager has, you may be worth the risk. They have life experience (that's why they are managers) and they know that sometimes a salesperson wasn't a good fit with a product or territory in a past position, but if the candidate can show that they've learned something and bring the right skills to a new position, they can be effective. They know that sometimes personality conflicts can cost someone a job, but if they display energy, enthusiasm and seem like a good match for the new position it might be worth the risk to hire them anyway. People can change, and sometimes people who have been through difficult circumstances and have learned from them might be more useful than someone who hasn't graduated from the school of hard knocks. But the burden is going to be on you to show the potential employer why your past failures have made you more useful, not less.

On the other hand, sometimes you just have to accept the consequences of your actions and adjust your career goals. If you embezzled from a former employer or abused a subordinate, it's unlikely that anyone is ever going to give you a position where you can do those things again. You may need to truly reexamine your life and work and retrain yourself for other jobs where you can have the opportunity to succeed.

One way to rehabilitate your career after a failure is through volunteering. If you've done something criminal then it's important that you be very transparent with the volunteer organization for their sake and yours. If your mistakes were based on inexperience or poor judgment or immaturity, then volunteer work can be a way to demonstrate that you have grown and can work with others constructively. It can provide you with new references and new skill sets.

●　　●　　●

The story of your career that you tell on your resume is perhaps your primary tool in your job search. It can open doors: I have seen candidates be given extraordinary interview opportunities because their story was so compelling and well-told. It can also slam doors in your face, as we saw in the case of Aleksey Vayner's video resume. You must invest significant effort and get significant help in writing the most effective resume possible.

Many job-seekers pay hefty fees to professional resume writing services. In my experience this is almost always a waste of money, and probably counter-productive. Most resume writing services have little or no experience in the hiring process. They never work with their clients over an extended period of time to see the results of their work or to measure the impact of their writing. Over my two decades of preparing and placing candidates in jobs all around the world, I have tracked the results of the resumes

I have helped them submit. I have learned what worked and what didn't, how to craft a resume that gets callbacks and how to predict which ones will cause the candidate's phone *not* to ring. In the companion workbook to *The ReExamined Life,* I have included more specific tools and worksheets to assist you in putting these field-tested techniques to use. You only get one chance to tell your story to an employer, and it's worth it to spend the time to work with these tools to increase the odds that your story will connect.

❧ Chapter 10 ❧

Selling Yourself Without Selling Out

My friend's wife just calls it, "That horrible scene from that awful movie." She shudders with disgust.

The context: in the early 1990s my friend and his wife were living through another severe recession in Southern California. The aerospace industry had collapsed, leading to tens of thousands of layoffs and the ripple effect was pulling down housing values, etc. My friend had a background in academia, but the economic situation had led him to take a sales job with a national company. The base salary didn't quite cover their expenses and he needed sales commissions to keep the family in the black. The pressure of

sales was new to my friend, whose years in a
university environment left him bright and
pleasant but not quite aggressive enough to
compete in such tough times. The stress he and
his wife felt, fearing that they would eventually
lose their house unless he started closing deals,
was ratcheted up by the pressure being put on
him and the rest of the local sales staff by the
national office. He trudged off every day,
anxious and uncertain, trying to meet people
and make presentations, but had few results to
show for his efforts.

One of the new movies for rent at the video
store that year was *Glengarry Glen Ross.* The
story takes place over two days in the suburban
branch office of a real estate company and follows the half-dozen salesmen there as they
struggle to meet the sales quota imposed by the
owners. A warning: it's one of the most profan-
ity-rich movies you ever heard, and the bad language starts out early as actor Alec Baldwin
chews up the scenery and the rear-ends of the
salesmen in his only scene, at the beginning of
the film. Baldwin plays one of the corporation's
top sales managers, sent down from headquarters to deliver an ultimatum like a drill sergeant:
the top salesman that week will receive a new
Cadillac, the second place finisher will get a set
of steak knives and the rest will be fired. Baldwin berates them for their pathetic inability to
close a sale. Baldwin barks at one guy, "Put that
coffee down! Coffee is for closers only... you call
yourself a salesman?!" He tells all of them, "Only
one thing counts in this life: get them to sign on

the line which is dotted!" He hammers them to get out and sell aggressively with two acronyms on a blackboard: *A-B-C: Always Be Closing* and *A-I-D-A: Attention, Interest, Decision, Action.*

The salesmen, mostly easy-going and middle-aged, are thrown into a panic. Jack Lemmon's character hasn't made a sale in a while and desperately needs a commission check to pay his daughter's medical bills. The vicious verbal beating delivered by Baldwin doesn't genuinely motivate the men; instead, the film is a study of their anxiety and desperation. They plead for the fresh set of high-quality lead cards (the "Glengarry leads") that Baldwin dangles in front of them so that they can rush out and make sales presentations, pushing to close a deal before the deadline.

My friends remember renting the movie and settling down after the kids had gone to bed to relax, then feeling sick to their stomachs during Alec Baldwin's scene. It hit a raw nerve and brought all of the fear that they were feeling to a head. My friend's desperation at not being able to close a sale had begun to feed on itself: the more he pushed, the worse his results. His wife simply couldn't take it. She grabbed the remote and ejected the movie at the end of the Baldwin scene. They never saw the rest of the movie. It was just too close to home.

For most people, just one job interview is stressful. Interview after interview without success becomes frightful and depressing. They trudge out, like the salesmen in *Glengarry Glen*

Ross, trying to sell themselves, only to sit waiting by the phone for calls and offers that don't come. Their family and friends ask how the interviews went, and they can't answer because they don't know what they are doing wrong. They get scared and self-conscious. They wonder what's wrong with them. Most of us would rather do just about anything other than walk into another interview and try to close the deal on ourselves.

This chapter is about selling yourself in the interview process but I know that the last thing that most of you need is someone to play the Alec Baldwin character to you right now. You don't need clever little acronyms and snazzy formulas for how to sell yourself, reminders that "winners win with a winning attitude" and all of that. I don't want to provoke the same response in you that my friend's wife had when she ejected the movie and have you toss this book aside because it made you feel like a loser for not being able to "close the deal."

Instead, I want to suggest something that might surprise you in a book about job loss: interviews are not sales presentations. The purpose is not to go in and be whatever they want you to be, to schmooze your way into a job by laughing at lame jokes or shoveling insincere praise on the boss's bowling trophy. Yes, you need a job but you are not there to lie, manipulate, seduce or prostitute yourself for that job. You are not there to win the position at all costs.

An interview is a discovery process. Both

the employer and you have the same goal: to discover if you really are the solution to their problem.   If you aren't, no matter how much you
need that paycheck, it will end badly for both
you and the employer. Think of it from their
point of view. Right now they have a problem.
They hire you because they think that you're the
solution. Maybe that's because they didn't work
hard enough to find out if you really are the
solution, or because you were slick enough to
convince them that you are when you aren't.
Regardless, let's say that you get the job.   Now
one problem has grown to two: the original one
and you. You have become a new problem to the
company because you're the wrong person for
that position. That's bad for them and for you.
Sure, you get a paycheck... for a while.   But
when a round peg is jammed into a square hole
neither the peg nor the hole are going to be
happy.

I know, I know: at this point you'd be
thrilled to get any paycheck, regardless of
whether the job is a perfect fit or whether you're
happy there. I understand, and I'm not saying
that the interview process is like looking for a
soulmate, where your and the interviewer's eyes
are supposed to meet across a crowded room
and you both know that this was a match made
in the stars. What I'm saying is that if you see
the interview process as nothing more than a
sale to be made, then you will run three risks.
First, you can feel defeated like the salesmen in
Glengarry Glen Ross when you can't "close a
deal." Second, you run the risk of offending the

interviewer with what might come off as an insincere or aggressive manner. Third, you might
succeed in making a bad match, which will give
you a paycheck for a little while but result in
wasting months and furthering damaging your
resume when, inevitably, you don't work out in
the new position.

That doesn't mean that there is no selling
going on during the interview. Both you and the
company are presenting yourselves as positively
as possible in the hope that both of you will discover a mutually beneficial match. Exhibiting
basic business manners, courtesy and people
skills are not--and should never be seen--as a
technique for making a sale. Those are the
things that we owe each other out of simple re-
spect--the obligations of civilizations. If you only
switch on manners, courtesy and decent people
skills when you're trying to "sell," then I assume
that most of the time you are rude and inconsiderate. I hope that you don't get a job with my
organization, because I don't want to have to
have to work with you every day after you've
"closed the deal" with the hiring manager. As a
manager, whenever I've considered hiring
someone, I've always been turned off if I feel that
I'm being "sold." I wonder what they'll become
after I've bought them. That's what I want to
discover as a manager before I hire them.

Instead of thinking of the interview as a
sales presentation, I'd like for you to think of it
as a blind date. Both of you have heard about
the other, and now it's time to meet to see if
what intrigued both of you on paper leads to

personal chemistry. Be yourself--your best self, to be sure--but be yourself. Learn as much as you share to discover if you're interested in pursuing this. Find out where it goes. If it's working, great. If it's not, you can't make it work.

Presenting Yourself Positively

There are things that I shouldn't have to say because they are obvious, yet I see people ignore them constantly. For example: dress appropriately for the situation. I once had a candidate, a very bright engineer, who dressed and groomed himself like someone going to a Halloween party as a "nerd." His weirdly out–of–fashion clothes and "Prince Valiant" haircut turned heads whenever he walked into an office for an interview. He couldn't understand why he wasn't getting callbacks or offers, considering his accomplishments. After all, wouldn't he be able to solve the company's technical problems? What he failed to understand was that the way he presented himself made managers fear that while he might offer technical solutions, he also might create people problems. Most positions in modern companies, even in engineering departments, involve teamwork and interpersonal communication. I certainly didn't want him to sell himself insincerely, but I saw no reason for him to handicap himself in the interview process. I asked him to trust me and sent him to a local men's clothing shop that I had a relationship

with and then to a barber I knew. With a new
suit and a haircut, his next interview resulted in
an offer.

Does this contradict my earlier point about
not pretending to be someone that you are not?
What happens when, a couple of days into the
job, a guy like that goes back to wearing his own
clothes and growing his hair back out? If that
happens, then he didn't use the interview as an
opportunity for him to discover what the company's values and culture were. My goal in getting him a suit and a haircut was not just to
clean him up for the hiring manager; it was to
teach him something.   Hopefully he learned
about what it took to be a part of the company,
namely that beyond having technical expertise,
the employees there dressed and groomed
sharply. That interview was his opportunity to
discover whether they were a good fit for him,
not just the other way around. If he felt uncom-
fortable with their culture during the interview
then he shouldn't have taken the offer. But he
never would have learned that if he hadn't
presented himself positively enough to go in and
engage in the interview process.

By far, the most important factor in
presenting yourself positively is passion and energy. There are simple truths about human interaction, and one of them is that people respond to the energy level of the person that they
are speaking with. If your voice and demeanor
are positive and upbeat, if you project a serious
purpose with a light heart and a twinkle in your
eye, most people are going to adjust their energy

level to match yours. Again, I am not telling you to adopt an insincere tone in an attempt to sell a false image of yourself. What I am saying is that the employer is discovering who you are during the interview, and you want them to see the best of your energy and attitude on display. Not something fake or contrived, but not you at your most passive and tentative, either.

If we invite someone to visit our home, common sense and common courtesy indicates that we should pick up the newspapers up off the floor and not answer the door in our underwear and slippers. Common sense and common courtesy are the basic grease that allows people to work together. Displaying sense and courtesy in how you dress, speak and behave at an interview isn't selling, it's allowing the employer to discover that you have those qualities and that you would probably make use of them if you came to work in their business.

What I'm arguing for can be summed up as integrity. The integrity to be honest about who you are and the integrity to show sincere respect and interest in who the employer is. Integrity in an interview means that you value yourself and the employer enough to show respect for the occasion. It also means that you are genuinely curious about the employer and what they have to say, and not dominating the time with a "sales pitch" about yourself. It means not groping for superficial connections with the interviewer or showering them with meaningless compliments. Integrity in an interview means engaging in the process without allowing desperation or any other extreme emotions to control your thoughts, voice or mannerisms. It means both answering and asking questions fairly. If you present yourself as a positive and polite person, a problem solver with energy, passion and integrity, you will stand out among the candidates being interviewed for any job, no matter how many there are.

The Discovery Process

There are some mechanics to the interview process. There are questions that you should be prepared to answer and to ask, and if you haven't thought them through in advance, then you're simply unprepared. There are topics that you should try to steer the conversation toward and some that you should absolutely avoid. There are specific cultural cues that you should both give and look for. There are cultural rituals and best practices. The purpose of this book and this chapter isn't to provide that level of detail, but I walk through all of it in the workbook that accompanies *The ReExamined Life* and my DVD series. I encourage you to make use of those. There are some basic principles that should guide you through the interview, however.

Go Prepared. There really is no excuse for not preparing for the interview--absolutely none. If an employer calls you into an interview and you can't make the time or effort to prepare then, honestly, you don't deserve the job. In the companion workbook I provide a pre-interview checklist so that you can be certain that you are ready, but there are some items that should be obvious. Do you have a spare copy of your resume along? Your references? Have you reviewed your resume and rehearsed answers to questions that you will almost certainly be asked? I recently interviewed someone and asked him what I thought was a simple question: what did you do in your last position? Not where did you work or what was your title, but what did you actually do? He hesitated, fumbled, had to think about it for a minute and try again. How could he not be prepared to answer that question? Do not even consider going into an interview that prone to drop the ball. Are you prepared to review your accomplishments in a concise and confident way, without boasting? Are you ready to explain any problem areas in your career? You should actually rehearse the dialogue that you can anticipate, not only your answers but the questions that you want to ask the employer.

Know as Much About the Company as The Interviewer Does. You can act interested in the company during the interview, and you might even get away with it. Or you can be genuinely interested and not have to fake it. How do you show genuine interest to the interviewer? Research the company before going in. I have seen, over and over again throughout the years, that the one characteristic of people who ace their interviews and get offers is that they come into the company already knowing as much as, or in some cases more, about the business than the person conducting the interview.

One friend interviewed with a business that wasn't particularly large, maybe 500 employees, but was owned by a larger, national corporation. He went through the resume process and got called in for what was essentially a screening interview for a management job. The company had gotten several dozen applications for the position, and narrowed that down to maybe five or six that were called in for interviews with a Human Resources person. The purpose of the screening interview was to see the applicants face-to-face, rate them on their appearance, verbal skills and so forth. HR would then select two candidates that would be called in a second time for a more extensive interview with the immediate supervisor and the vice-president over the division that the open position was in. My friend had a few days to prepare for this screening interview and he used that time to research the company. He scoured their website and familiarized himself with their products, their pricing, history, markets. Just a few minutes with Google led him to articles about one of their premier products and speculation about the upgrade expected next year. Google gave him current and historical information about the company's stock price and that of the parent company. He was able to easily find articles about their major competitors and challenges that the industry faced. He followed links to more information about the parent company, and found on their website the previous year's annual stockholder report, which talked about the parent corporation's expansion strategy. He Googled the names of the company president and vice-presidents and found information about their careers and accomplishments. Finally, he used his social and professional networks to ask other people who worked there, or used to work there, or who worked for competitors or suppliers, to give him as much background as they could about the business, its strengths, weaknesses and challenges.

When the day for the screening interview came, he sat down in a small conference room in the Human Resources department with a member of their staff. The chairs in the HR lobby were full of other people waiting for their screening interviews. My friend aced his. When she asked about his accomplishments he responded by pointing out what he had done in the past would be relevant to the company, their products and the challenges of the industry. He asked her appropriate questions about how the department and position he was applying for would be affected by upcoming changes that had been discussed in so many articles that he found online. The woman conducting the interview smiled, tilted her head and said, "I don't know. That's something that you'll want to ask the vice-president when you meet with him." That's when he knew he had made it past the screening interview. When the final interview came a week later he had prepared even further, and that meeting ended up becoming less of an interview than it was a brainstorming session with his future boss and the vice-president about how they could solve the problems that the department was working through. He didn't have to *pretend* to be a problem solver; his knowledge about the company simply showed them that he *was* a problem solver, and the solution that they were looking for. Obviously, he got the job.

Make it a Conversation. Your interview isn't a quiz show, nor is it an interview in the way that a newspaper reporter asking a celebrity questions is an interview. Your interview should be a first meeting between you and the people that you hope to work for. It should be a conversation, a constructive give-and-take in which you ask as many questions as you answer. This is what I meant by a "process of discovery," as both sides try to find out if the two of you are a good match. I will often ask someone after an interview if they had found out exactly what they would do, who they would work for or how much travel would be involved. Too many times I have and been told, "I'm not sure, we didn't really talk about that." If so, then it was a missed opportunity for that person to discover whether the job would be a good fit for them. If they do get an offer it might answer some of their questions, especially the compensation, but an offer letter or phone call is unlikely to give them all the information they need to make a well-informed decision. They had that opportunity in the interview and they didn't take it. You should go into an interview with a list of questions that you need to get answered and tactfully work through them. If the company is unable or unwilling to tell you want you need to know to be able to commit yourself to their team it might be a sign that you won't ever feel comfortable there.

There is another important reason to make the interview a conversation: it demonstrates to the interviewer that you can work with others. If you are passive and only answer direct questions while nodding your head occasionally, you won't give the impression that you will be able to engage and participate as a member of a team. The interviewer might wonder if this is your normal mode in meetings and over the phone: when working with other employees or customers will you ask questions if you need more information? Will you be passive and not voluntarily contribute to the group's knowledge? They are trying to discover who you are, not play Twenty Questions or dig responses out of you. If you can put the interviewer at ease, engage in an easy and productive conversation in that setting, it's a good indication of what type of employee you might be.

Knowing When to Walk Away

If the interview is a discovery process, a sort of "first date," then you should be prepared to discover that it isn't a good match. Certainly the employer is prepared to discover through the interview that you aren't the person that they

are looking for. Yet the unemployed person often
feels so desperate for a job, any job, that they
haven't considered the possibility that during
the interview they might discover that *this* job
would be wrong for them. When the conversation
is going badly the candidate's temptation is to
start trying to please the interviewer, saying
whatever they think that will win the job for
them.

Here's a hard truth: sometimes the wrong
job is worse than no job at all. You might get a
paycheck, for a little while, until it becomes ap-
parent to both parties that it isn't working out.
In the meantime you might make yourself and
everyone around you miserable, waste weeks or
months that could have been spent looking for
the right job and put a failure as the most recently held slot on your resume. Walking away
can be a sign of either immaturity or maturity,
depending on your motivations. I'm not talking
about turning your nose up because you think
that the position is beneath you or storming off
in a snit because you don't get everything that
you think you want or deserve. I'm talking
about having the self-awareness to know when
something will not be right for you and the confidence to keep looking for another job rather
than put yourself in a situation where you cannot succeed or be happy. To illustrate, let me
give you personal examples from the two guys
writing this book.

Early in my career I went through a personal tragedy: my brother took his own life while I

was living in Florida, working as an accountant. I felt that I needed to move back to Michigan to be closer to my parents and siblings through the aftermath of that event. I interviewed with an accounting firm that was hiring a tax manager in the area where I wanted to relocate. At that point I had had significant experience in forensic accounting (preparing tax law cases for court) and during the interview I pushed my litigation experience. The company was looking for someone to prepare tax returns, and it became clear in the interview that they had no interest in forensic accounting. Like a woman who marries a man that she knows is wrong for her because she thinks that she can change him, I thought that if I took the position that over time I could change it, shaping it to suit my needs and wants, and become this firm's "litigation guy." Instead of honest answers to the interviewer's questions, I told him what I thought he wanted to hear and presented myself as someone who couldn't wait to file a pile of tax returns. I wanted the job for family reasons, and also because I had dreams of moving back home, making big bucks, eventually leaving and starting my own business. In short, I wanted the job for all the wrong reasons, but I wasn't honest with them or myself about that. I got the job and on the first day, within my first thirty minutes in the new office, I knew that I'd made a terrible mistake. I began trying to find a way to make it work, or get out, but I was a round peg in a square hole. It took me eight painful months to get fired. Through the interview process I had discovered what I needed to know, but I didn't have the maturity or courage to walk away.

My co-author Greg has a Master of Divinity degree (the professional degree qualifying someone to be a Protestant pastor) and additional post-graduate education beyond that. He spent the first ten years of his career as a pastor but in his early thirties he left his church to pursue a career as a writer and creative consultant. After a while, as the country was going through another recession, his business was drying up and he needed a job. He networked, sent out resumes, went through the big job placement websites, but the job market was tight and he wasn't finding anything. He was burning through his savings and worried about his family. One day he interviewed for a position selling insurance. He had friends in this line of work and knew that it could be a great job for the right person, so he drove to the address he had been given with a hopeful attitude. He waited in the lobby, watching the employees shuffle in and out, anxious and unsmiling. When he was called back into the company owner's office Greg was taken aback by his insincere, aggressive manner. Greg remembers him as being almost exactly like the Alec Baldwin character in Glengarry Glen Ross. The owner didn't ask Greg many questions, instead giving a sales pitch for the company and talking about how much money that he made. Apparently, the business consisted of selling temporary insurance to migrant workers who spoke little English, closing deals fast and getting cash payment from them if possible. Greg remembers the guy telling him that if he took the job, he would go to construction sites and farms during the harvest season and, "Sign them up on the spot, right over the hood of a pickup truck."

Greg looked at his shoes and drifted off in thought. He remembered his teachers, who had encouraged him to do something to make the world a better place. He thought about the years he had spent as a pastor, the troubles he had seen people go through, the ways he had tried to help them. He thought about his kids, and what he taught them about making whatever you do for a living something of value for others. He thought about migrant workers that he had known and mission work he had done with them. He tried to imagine himself leaning over the hood of a pickup truck, trying to do a "hard close" and getting a migrant who was trying to save money to wire home to his children in Honduras to sign an insurance policy written in small print in a language he didn't understand. As Greg told me, "I looked into the Abyss, and realized that for me there were worse things than being unemployed and maybe even losing my house." Apparently he had been so lost in thought that he hadn't heard the company owner ask him a question, and now the guy was barking at him to respond. Greg looked up and said, "I'm sorry, I'm not supposed to be here. I'm not interested in the position. I'm sorry for wasting your time." He got up and walked out. Greg had discovered that it would have been the wrong job for him, and no matter how badly he needed the money, he wouldn't do anyone any good by trying to do something that he wasn't cut out for.

• • •

An interview is not, and shouldn't be, a sales pitch. The company shouldn't be trying to sell you a job, nor should you be trying to sell yourself to them. It should be an honest conversation, a process in which both parties attempt to discover whether the two of you would be a good match. Of course, everyone presents their features and benefits and is professional and courteous. But the pressure of trying to "close a deal" leads to mistakes. It causes companies urgently needing to hire someone to pick the wrong candidate and create a whole new set of problems for themselves. It causes candidates not to be honest with themselves or the interviewer and to set themselves up for the next bad chapter in their career. It causes those who don't get the offer to feel personally rejected, like losers who couldn't sell themselves. If everyone involved in the interview process saw it instead as a chance to learn, it would remove the element of "failure" from the equation. Bad matches are bad matches, and if all parties could recognize that, then they could move on to matching the right person with the right job.

❧ Chapter 11 ❧

Shape, Don't be Shaped By, Your World

HIGGINS:
*In Hartford, Hereford and Hampshire
Hurricanes Hardly Ever Happen.*

ELIZA:
*In 'artford, 'ereford and 'ampshire
'urricanes 'ardly ever 'appen.*

The Academy Award for Best Picture in 1964 went to *My Fair Lady,* along with seven other Oscars. It is the story of Henry Higgins, a professor of Phonetics (the study of pronunciation) and a poor young woman named Eliza Doolittle who sells flowers in

the streets of London. Professor Higgins is an
arrogant English aristocrat who believes that
people's accents—their pronunciation tones
when speaking—determine their prospects in society. In other words, Higgins believes that the
poor are doomed to poverty because they cannot
speak well enough to advance to the upper
classes. He wagers another a friend of his that
by using his techniques he can teach any woman from the streets to speak well enough to be
passed off as a duchess at the upcoming Em-
bassy Ball. Eliza is chosen as the test subject,
and in the scene quoted above Higgins is trying
to break her Cockney (working-class London) ac-
cent which drops the "H" sound at the beginning
of words. By the end of the film Higgins has
transformed Eliza from a Cockney street vendor
into a woman who moves at ease within aristo-
cratic society.

Most fans of the movie know that it was an
adaptation from a Broadway stage musical of the
same name. What fewer people realize is that
the musical was itself an adaptation of an earlier
play by George Bernard Shaw, called *Pygmalion.*
Shaw published his clever and witty play in
1912, but underlying it were serious issues that
troubled late 19th century Britain. During that
century the Industrial Revolution and urbaniza-
tion created a huge underclass. The cities were
full of terrible slums, and both the factories and
the mines that supplied them used armies of
child laborers. The mean streets of London that
Charles Dickens wrote about in his novels were
quite real, and many people in England began to

think and write about the urban poor and the probable fate of the "street urchins" that they saw everywhere. At the same time, Charles Darwin wrote a book that changed the world, *The Origin of Species*, introducing the idea of Evolution.

All this and other influences combined to foster an idea in late 19th and early 20th century England called S*ocial Darwinism,* or S*ocial Determinism.* The notion was that people were doomed to be merely products of their environment and class. According to this line of reasoning poverty, underemployment or unemployment produced certain types of people: cunning (in the ways of survival) but not clever; mean-spirited not generous; violent not refined. Unemployment (or underemployment) made one crude, bitter, unable to speak well, wary of strangers or other cultures, incapable of entrepreneurship or leadership. It robbed one of the ability to appreciate art, culture or literature. Some aristocrats saw it as their burden to reach down and help the poor, bitter underclass by sharing bits of their wisdom and culture. They figured that the victims of Britain's cycles of economic change were hopeless without the work of do-gooders like them. The back-story of *My Fair Lady* is a reflection upon what is possible for the unemployed and underemployed, just like this book.

What's interesting about *Pygmalion* is Shaw's notion that someone's language could raise their station in life. Eliza Doolittle's life is changed because she learns to speak differently. Not only does she start pronouncing the "H's" at

the beginning of words, she learns to express
herself moderately, with discretion. In a memor-
able scene she relapses when Higgins takes her
to Ascot, the famous horse racing track for British high society, and in her excitement she for-
gets who she is trying to be and reverts to the
habits of the street, shouting at the horse to,
"Move your bloomin' arse!" Nevertheless, by the
end of the film Eliza has learned to speak well,
display proper manners and be gracious to others. Those things change not only her life but
her fortunes.

You Do Not Have to Be a Victim
of Unemployment

Today I had coffee with a sixty year old man
who is unemployed and has no retirement savings. I'm meeting a lot of people like that these
days. In today's economy people are losing not
only jobs but homes and retirement accounts.
What will happen to them?

Are they doomed to become an embittered
underclass? Must they be angry or unable to
experience beautiful things in life? Is it inevit-
able that they will be hostile to immigrants, giv-
en to ranting on the Internet or selfishly clinging
to what little they have and not sharing it with
the world unless do-gooders from the upper
classes show them how?

No.

I completely reject not only those notions
but even the premise that they are based on.

They do not have to be victims, any more than Eliza Doolittle was doomed to selling flowers on the street and dropping her "H's." They need not be mere products of their environment; they can shape their worlds and their lives.

You do not have to be a victim of your unemployment. You can decide what kind of person you will be, what kind of life you will have and what kind of world you will live in. You can do it by changing the same things that Higgins changed in Eliza: how you speak, how you behave and how you give.

"Pleasant Words are a Honeycomb"

How well do you speak? I'm not only asking whether you use proper grammar and pronunciation—although that does matter, especially in a job search—but do you speak well: well of others, well of the world around you, well of your situation, well of yourself?

Language has tremendous power to shape our perceptions. How we describe a person, place or thing—what we name it—often controls how we understand it. In politics both sides try be the first to name problems or proposed solutions, because they understand that what a law or government program gets called, especially in the media, shapes public perceptions of it. Medical patients often feel better once a diagnosis is

made because it gives a name to what is wrong
with them.   In the Bible, Adam is given the
power to name, or define, the animals.   In fact,
many people in the Bible are given new names to
signify some change in their identity, or to create a change in their identity. God renames Ab-
ram *Abraham,* which means "Father of Many Na-
tions." God gives Jacob the new name *Israel,*
which means "He Who Wrestles with God."
When the boy Daniel, whose name in Hebrew
means "Judged by (the) God (of Israel)," is taken
into captivity by the Babylonians, he is renamed
Belteshazzar, which indicates he is from then to
be known as a "Prince of Baal (one of the Baby-
lonian gods)."   In the classic Johnny Cash song,
A Boy Named Sue, a father gives his son a girl's
name because it will cause all the other boys to
pick on him and force him to grow up tough.
Names matter.

How are you describing things in your unemployment?   What names are you giving to
former employers, your career, your financial
situation, your prospects, your skills, possible
jobs, people around you?   Just in the last week
I've spoken to several people in their fifties who
are unemployed, have lost most or all of the
equity in their homes and have seen their pen-
sions or retirement accounts basically wiped
out.   All of them were planning on retiring sometime in the next decade or so and spending the
following twenty or thirty years enjoying themselves.   I've been struck by the different language that they used to describe their situations.   One guy sees himself as "screwed."   He

"has nothing." There are "no jobs for an old guy" like him. He "has to get a crummy job" because his house is "a boat anchor" around his neck. Another guy—almost identical circumstances—admits that he has "challenges" but sees "opportunities" not problems. He and his wife now have an "opportunity" to start a small business that they've always dreamed of and "twenty five years to grow it into something." They see this as the "beginning of a new life" that reminds them of when they first got married. As for the house, they're thankful that they have one, but "it's just a house" and "home is wherever we make a life." Another guy I talked to said that he and his wife have always dreamed of becoming missionaries. They see this time as an "opportunity" to follow that dream "ahead of schedule" and are considering moving to work in a school/hospital in the mountains of Central America.

I just Googled the phrase "positive language" and Google listed 65,900 pages on the Web that mention those terms. In the last few years the business world, educational institutions and self-help books have been buzzing about the power of positive language to shape perceptions and behaviors. It's easy to roll one's eyes and dismiss it all as happy talk for a feel-good culture. I know several people who reject any suggestion that they use more positive language because of political correctness and pop psychology from the Age of Aquarius.

One would be hard-pressed to describe ancient Israel as "politically correct" or the Old

Testament as a feel-good self-help book. But the Bible frequently talks about the power of language to shape our lives. Take the Book of Proverbs, for example. It makes clear distinctions between the speech of a wise man and the speech of "the fool." Consider Proverbs 16:23-24:

> *A wise man's heart guides his mouth, and his lips promote instruction. Pleasant words are a honeycomb, sweet to the soul and healing to the bones.*

The point is that the wise man uses language to not only instruct but to nourish himself and those around him. In the examples I gave above of the fifty-somethings facing unemployment and delayed retirements, which ones do you think provided useful instruction and healing, down into the bones, for themselves and their families?

Wise and good words spring from a wise and good heart. Words from that kind of heart is gracious: not flattering or dishonest, but gracious. This kind of speech not only focuses on opportunities rather than problems, it creates opportunities for that person. A person who speaks positively will advance in society, just as Eliza Doolittle did in *My Fair Lady*. I guarantee that an unemployed person who speaks this way will have vastly more job prospects and a exponentially more successful job search than the person who names and frames everything negatively.   Think that's pop-psychology?   Consider Proverbs 22:11:

> *He who loves a pure heart and whose speech is gracious will have the king for his friend.*

The unemployed person who chooses to rant about their problems or speak about everything in negative or derogatory terms only makes a bad situation worse, and risks making their problems permanent features of their life. Proverbs 10:10:

> *A chattering fool comes to ruin. The mouth of the righteous is a fountain of life, but violence overwhelms the mouth of the wicked.*

An unemployed person who speaks negatively, without thinking about the effect that their words might have on family, friends or their personal and professional networks, wounds and divides the people around them, driving away loved ones, colleagues and business opportunities. Proverbs 12:18 and 18:6-7:

> *Reckless words pierce like a sword, but the tongue of the wise brings healing... A fool's lips bring him strife... his mouth is his undoing, and his lips are a snare to his soul.*

The New Testament Book of James describes the tongue as one of our smallest but most dangerous parts. It can, James says, both praise and curse. We must be always cautious, because our tongues and the words they produce can lead us places that we don't want to go. James says that they are like the bit in a horse's mouth, or the rudder on a ship, or a small spark that sets a giant forest on fire. As an unemployed person, searching for direction, you must understand that your words can choose your direction for you. Negative, critical, hostile, pessimistic and ranting language might not only keep you un- or underemployed, it can ruin your relationships and leave you to stew in your own misery. Proverbs 17:27:

> *A man of knowledge uses words with restraint, and a man of understanding is even-tempered.*

"Manners Maketh the Man"

We've all seen this portrayed so often in film and television that we can all imagine the scene. A bus pulls up in front of some low buildings and young men—and more often, young women, as well—file out while a sergeant shouts at them to form a line. The sergeant berates them for the ineptness of their line and bemoans that this is, without a doubt, the worst group of recruits that he has ever been forced to set his eyes upon. Over the next few hours they get new haircuts, clothes and routines. They are exercised relentlessly, taught how and when to salute, who to apply the term, "Sir" to and who to never call "Sir" (i.e., the sergeant, who will yell back, "Don't call me 'Sir.' I work for a living!"). A few months later their families come to their graduation, and moms and dads don't recognize their own child when they march out onto the tarmac. They have been transformed from the kid that they knew into something else: United States Marines.

The Marine Corps knows the same thing that William of Wykeham, the English Bishop of Winchester in the 14th century, knew. In addition to building Windsor Castle (he was such a successful architect that he was promoted to bishop) he was famous for saying, and placing on his coat of arms, the statement: *Manners Makyth Man,* famously remembered as the truism that *Manners Maketh the Man.* It's true that who we are springs from our heart, but William of Wykeham and the Corps both knew that teaching someone standards and codes of behavior usually modifies their actual behavior. Earlier in this book we talked about how amazingly calm under stress Captain "Sully" was as he landed US Airways Flight 1549 successfully on the Hudson River. What we may not remember was that "Sully" graduated with honors from the United States Air Force Academy. Standards and codes of conduct had been so ingrained into him at an early age that they are simply part of who he is. He doesn't have to *remind* himself to behave in a certain way in the cockpit, he just *does.* Manners make the man, and they matter to the unemployed person for two reasons.

First, like your language, your manners

shape your world. The quality of your life experience is closely linked to your personal conduct, your daily routine, dress, hygiene, housekeeping, communications, interactions with others and financial habits. If you live in a disorganized, lazy and inconsiderate manner, you will, almost by definition, have a life that reflects that. If you act like a slob then it's likely that you are a slob, and your life and career will be slob-like. I've spent lot of time doing mission work in some of the poorest countries on earth, like Haiti. Even in the worst of economic times America's standard of living and opportunities are orders of magnitude greater than in these places. Yet even in the poorest communities I still see some families that keep their homes and clothes immaculately clean. They may live in a one-room shack without indoor plumbing or glass in the windows, and their furniture may be cast-off plastic lawn chairs, but they are kept as clean and neat as any home anywhere. The nicest clothes that the family owns may be the children's school uniforms, but when the kids walk the dirt streets to school their shirts are pressed and starched and bright white. They may be poor, but they don't let the poverty of their circumstances shape their manners. Their manners and behavior shape their life and world. What will drive your experience during this chapter in your life: your manners or your unemployment?

The second reason why manners matter to the unemployed is a hard truth: when the economy is roaring and employers need warm bodies to fill slots, they'll hire and keep slobs. Even rude slobs. When the economy is in rough seas, the slobs go overboard. Especially the rude ones. Networking and job searching during a recession is an uphill battle even if you make a good impression. If you make a bad impression on the people that you meet then it can be nearly impossible to compete for a good job. At a *ReExamine Life* workshop that I did recently a man was complaining that he was getting nowhere in his job search. The guy was wearing worn cowboy boots and jeans, a black t-shirt with cigarettes in the sleeve, had hair below his shoulders and a long, scraggly beard. The outfit was topped by a big cowboy hat with a feather. Now that might be quite the style for a country western star, but this guy didn't seem like he put much effort into personal hygiene or laundry. He told me that he had been going into businesses and asking for a job but that when he was offered one for less than he thought that he should make he, "Gave them a piece of my mind!" I was honest with him: unless he wanted to work on a ranch or play back up in a honky-tonk band, not too many businesses want a Willie Nelson or Hank Williams, Jr. wannabe working in their Purchasing Department.

In *My Fair Lady* Eliza Doolittle didn't just learn to stop dropping her "H's," she learned the manners of polite society. If you moved to another country you would be wise to learn the customs and manners of that society, if you want to advance within it. In the same way, when you are unemployed with limited options your manners can not only shape your life, they can open doors.

Make a Life, Not a Living

When you are unemployed, your need for a job is always staring you in the face. The broken car that you can't afford to fix, the child's tuition payment that you can't make, the health insurance that you simply can't afford, period. If you're following my advice in this book, your days are now so full of networking, job searching and working temporary or odd jobs that you have less time today then you did when you were fully employed. You certainly have less money. It's easy to become so absorbed in your various efforts that you become self-centered. That's what those aristocrats in Victorian England thought about the lower classes: they could cunningly hustle for their own survival, but were incapable of thinking beyond themselves. They assumed that unemployment or underemployment breeds selfishness and intolerance. They assumed that since the lower classes grub for their daily bread, they must be incapable of great thoughts or great actions. The do-gooders from the upper classes figured that they must provide for them and lead them.

I agree that people who are obsessed with scrambling after enough money for all their wants and needs are selfish and intolerant. It almost goes without saying that if your every waking thought is about yourself—your job, your cash, your house, your food, your clothing, your car—then you have no room in your heart, mind or soul for anyone else. Your life is poor. But I do not agree that such people are always the un-employed or underemployed or working class or poor. I have known plenty of wealthy people in my life, and even more that want to be wealthy. Some of them had the most self-obsessed and self-absorbed and self-directed lives that I've ever seen. The opposite is also true: I've known many rich people who were humble, considerate and generous. I've seen the same contrasts in the poor, the underemployed and the unem-ployed. In fact, I've never seen any correlation between someone's generosity and concern for others and their income. Kind, thoughtful and giving people have lives that reflect that, regard-less of whether they make $30,000 or $300,000 per year.

Winston Churchill said, "We make a living by what we get, but we make a life by what we give." Your period of unemployment can be a season of selfish obsession over your own needs, but it doesn't have to be. It shouldn't be. If your heart is soft and gracious, if you genuinely care about other people—especially those around you—then there is no reason that any of those qualities have to stop while you are between jobs, or even if you find yourself start-ing over again at sixty years old.

I'm going to explore the topic of giving more thoroughly in the next chapter, but let's take a moment to reflect on that quote by Churchill. Throughout this chapter we've been talking about how what you say and the way you behave

frees you from victim-hood. Your life doesn't
have to be a reflection of your circumstances; instead, your circumstances can reflect your life.
I'm not saying that you can simply "think and
grow rich" or any such nonsense. What it
means is that you can have joy and dignity regardless of how much money you make, where
you live or what you do for a living. You can
bless the people around you with your words
and manners. These are the building blocks of a
life worth living, as we've talked about all
through this book. Churchill reminds us that
while we make a living with our work, we make a
worthy life by caring for others, by giving what
we can to them, by sharing whatever we have to
build a legacy and make the world around us
better. You may not be able to cure AIDS or feed
the hungry in Africa or donate a new wing to the
hospital, but you can impact the lives of people
around you. Mother Theresa, who I wrote about
earlier in this book, said, "If you can't feed a
hundred people, then just feed one." She also
said, "We cannot do great things on this Earth,
only small things with great love." That is how
you stop working for a living, and start working
for a life that is worth living.

•   •   •

In early April of 2008, during the Demo-
cratic presidential primary campaign, Barack
Obama commented to an audience at a fun-
draiser in San Francisco that many people in the

small towns of Western Pennsylvania had become frustrated by job losses. "It's not surprising, then," said Obama, "[That] they get bitter, they cling to guns or religion or antipathy to people who aren't like them, or anti-immigrant sentiment or anti-trade sentiment as a way to explain their frustrations."

Obama was making, in effect, the same argument that some in late 19th century England made: a person's social and economic situation determines a person's attitudes and values. From this point of view, since you lost your job, you are likely to become bitter and escape your troubles with religion, lose compassion for others or take out your anger over your unemployment on immigrants or those less fortunate than you. Some people, whether they are Victorians in England or San Franciscans in Victorian mansions, figure that the street urchins of 19th century London or the unemployed of 21st century American must be miserable, with miserable lives. This may reveal more about them than the unemployed: perhaps it's how they imagine that they would feel in similar circumstances.

What they think about you doesn't matter. What they think that your life and world must be like is irrelevant. You can choose to speak well, hold yourself to high standards of conduct and give generously to those around you, employed or not. If you do, your world will be rich, even if you aren't.

❧ Chapter 12 ❦

Certain Unalienable Rights

T he first sign of trouble was that the big banks started failing.

The Federal government had borrowed huge sums of money over the previous seven years or so to fund expansion and an expensive war. The primary source of capital growth was government-held mortgages. The Federal government used those mortgages as collateral for its borrowing, and banks across the country showed healthy balance sheets because their assets were inflated by these mortgage-backed government securities. Speculators began doing what speculators do: they speculated on these banks, and recruited businesses and small investors to put their money in as well. With Federal-backed mortgage securities, it was practically a sure thing, wasn't it? Fortunes were made, on paper, and the investor class were the idols of the decade.

This wasn't 2009, or even 1929: it was 1819. What became known as the Panic of 1819 had its roots in the massive debt run up by the Federal government for the Louisiana Purchase, the growth of government following it, and the War of 1812. At the time it wasn't seen as a problem since the solution was so simple: the government would just sell some of the vast new tracts of land to settlers, who would start family farms and make mortgage payments. Of course many tracts were bought by land speculators who borrowed to buy them, planning to "flip" the real estate for a profit to new settlers, usually immigrants. The Federal government then took these mortgages and used them as security to borrow from the large national banks of the day. Everybody won, everybody got rich.

There were warnings. Thomas Jefferson, who had written the Declaration of Independence and had served as either Vice President or President from 1797 to 1809, said in 1814 that, "We are to be ruined by paper, as we were formerly by the old Continental paper." In 1816 he predicted that, "We are under a bank bubble" that would soon burst. A government-controlled bank was set up to stabilize the financial system, but it was grossly mismanaged. The federal regulators didn't limit the money supply; instead, they inflated it by making huge, new loans that fueled even more speculation. The federal and state banking systems were riddled with incompetence and fraud. Dozens of members of Congress held stock in these quasi-government banks and blocked any attempt to reel them in.

The tipping point came when the real estate bubble burst. People were unable to keep up with the mortgage payments on all of that land they had bought out west. Besides, there was so much new land always becoming available through westward expansion that the property values couldn't hold up. All that paper became nearly worthless.

When the Panic of 1819 started there were runs on the banks, thousands of which failed. Credit instantly dried up and nobody could get a loan. Those who had bought government land defaulted on their mortgages and the debt shifted to those who hadn't speculated. Businesses started going bankrupt and hundreds of thousands became unemployed (equivalent to millions today). In some Eastern cities like Philadelphia, the unemployment rate was reportedly over 50 percent and thousands were put into debtor's prison. On the outskirts of Baltimore, the unemployed lived in tent cities.

Only 43 years earlier Thomas Jefferson had written the Declaration of Independence, arguing to the world that men, *"Are endowed by their Creator with certain unalienable Rights, that among these are Life, Liberty and the pursuit of*

Happiness." It was, the Declaration continued, *"to secure these rights [that] Governments are instituted among Men, deriving their just powers from the consent of the governed."* Now an aged Jefferson bitterly reflected that the new generation "[Has] nothing in them of the feelings or principles of '76, [and] now look to a single and splendid government of an aristocracy, founded on banking institutions, and money incorporations... riding and ruling over the plundered ploughman and beggared yeomanry."

The Panic of 1819 was America's first genuine economic depression. It lasted about five years, until the engine of westward expansion drove growth for a thirteen year run, until the Panic of 1837. That lasted about six years and was followed by fourteen years of growth until the Panic of 1857. The Civil War lasted from 1861 to 1865, which was followed by growth until the Panics of 1873, 1893 and 1907. After that we began calling these cycles "recessions," with the recessions of 1918 and 1929 (which led to the Great Depression). The United States experienced recessions in 1953, 1957, 1960, 1973, 1980, 1990, and 2001.

What goes around comes around. The most recent one began, of course, in 2008 and has obvious parallels to the Panic of 1819. It's interesting to discuss what we may have learned, what might happen and how it could affect the economy in the future. But that's not the purpose of this book.

The purpose of this book is to point out

what is possible after you lose your job, so let's
be honest: neither you nor I have any control
over the macroeconomic cycles of history. We
can't predict them, other than to note that they
have come, on average, about every dozen years
in United States history. We can see the warning signs like clouds on the horizon, but you and
I can't prevent them any more than we can stop
a tornado. Since you've lost your job, and
maybe more than that, you feel especially power-
less before the relentless grind of global macroe-
conomies.

Here's what's possible for you, right now:
despite your unemployment and the cycles of
history, you can claim your right to life, liberty
and the pursuit of happiness. Rant and rave at
the politicians and bankers all that you want,
vote however you think best in the next election.
But you have the power—right now, today—to
reexamine the premise of your life and to stop
working merely to make a living. You can
choose to work for a life that is worth living. It
really is up to you.

The Right to Life

We've talked throughout this book about
having a life that is *worth* living. We talked
about what a valuable thing that life is and that
you can choose for it to be significant and gracious. In the last chapter I quoted Winston
Churchill, who said that, "We make a living by
what we get, but we make a life by what we
give." I want to say something more about that.

What are you giving? What are you willing
to give? I'm not talking about taking the pants
that don't fit to the thrift store so that you can
write six bucks off on your tax return. I'm talking about really giving some of your time and
money and possessions to either those less fortunate than yourself or to organizations that
make the world a better place. More than that:
what are you giving, or willing to give, to God?

Let me tell you about something that
happened at my church in West Michigan, just
yesterday. A couple of women from a church in
Detroit, on the other side of the state, came over
to our congregation in Holland to tell a story
about one of our members that most of us didn't
know. There's a fifty-something guy in our
church who lost his job, then lost his house. He
bought a used panel truck and started a small
business, running last-minute batches of parts
across the state from the suppliers in West
Michigan to the auto plants in Detroit. Sections
of the Detroit area have been economically dev-
astated. The collapse of the auto industry has
combined with other trends to create zones of
poverty that some of us never imagined possible
in a major American city. My friend was just a
guy trying to make enough bucks to keep it together. But as he drove through the Detroit
area, running parts in his panel truck, he saw
poor people with no coats in cold weather. He
didn't ask anybody, he didn't take the time to
work through an organization, he just started
asking everyone that he knew if they had any old
winter clothes that he could throw in his truck,

stuffed around his load. He'd make his delivery to the auto plant and then drive down to a corner in the worst part of Detroit, roll up the back of the truck and start handing out sweaters, jackets, hats and gloves to anyone who needed them. After a few weeks of this, a local prostitute visiting a soup-kitchen at a local church mentioned to the sisters who ran it that a tall, crazy, white man was handing out clothes on a corner, surrounded by pimps, drug dealers and gang members. The sisters rushed down, afraid that he'd get murdered for his truck. They began to work with him, providing a means through their church to more safely and effectively distribute the clothing.

He could have complained that he had lost his job, that he was a victim of the economy and collapse of the auto industry. He could have demanded that the government do something. But he saw cold people and he figured that he could help. So he did. Just like that. The two women who came over from Detroit yesterday thanked us. I really had no idea, but I knew that my friend was the kind of person who never thinks of himself as a victim, always does the right thing and knows that God expects us to care for the poor.

In fact, if we all cared for the poor, the widow, the orphan and the elderly like the Bible tells us to then we wouldn't need a bloated tax system to confiscate our earnings to do it for us. We have delegated our compassion to the government.

And that brings me to the subject of money. Here's the deal: God calls us to give money. Yes, we should volunteer; yes, we should donate old clothes; yes, we should teach a child to read, and all of that. But God has a lot to say about our money. Not because God needs our money (what does God need your money for?) but because He knows that how you feel about and use your money affects your heart. If God wanted to feed the poor He could drop money from the sky, or have oil gush from their back yard or make a million dollar banking error in their favor. But what kind of people would that create? What kind of world would that be?

Instead, He told us to give. When I sat down to write this book I understood the basic flaw in its business plan: why am I trying to sell books to unemployed people who have no money? Still, I believed that I could provide enough value through this book to make it worth your while to buy it. If that's so, how much more so is it true that God has so much more value to provide if you will give to him?

I used to work for the Internal Revenue Service. Yes, the dreaded IRS. We were the keepers of the secrets: we knew how much people made, how much they spent, how much they gave. Want to know a secret? In America, the people who give the most as a percentage of income are those who make the least. The IRS keeps statistics, and that data shows that the poor give more, out of their poverty, than the middle class or rich. If you're thinking that you would give more if you made more, then you are lying to yourself. It just doesn't work that way in reality. The more that people make, the more that they spend, the more that they are invested in the world and the less generous their hearts are to God or other people.

You can choose to give, and you should choose to. Give to your local church, and if you don't belong to one, give to a worthy charity. In fact, God challenges you to tithe.

That's certain to raise the ire of some unemployed folks. The notion that you should tithe—give ten percent of your income--when you're unemployed seems absurd. But it's something that I've practiced for years. Whatever check or income comes in, I give ten percent to my local church. God has always blessed that. I don't give in order to get. It isn't some sort of spiritual prosperity scheme. Instead, I trust God when he says in the Bible that a portion of my heart, my life and my money belong to him. When I invert the formula I feel grateful: everything—and I do mean everything— that I have belongs to God, and he lets me keep ninety percent of it for my own use. Even though I don't tithe in order to get a return, I believe that God honors those that honor him and that everything that I devote to him is returned many times over in this life and the next.

The Declaration of Independence tells us that Americans have a right to life. One way that we can claim that right is to live richly and abundantly. Read the third chapter of the Old Testament Book of Malachi. God challenges us to test him: give Him a tithe of all that you have and see how He blesses your life.

The Right to Liberty

The United States was founded on the rationale that you are endowed by your Creator with certain unalienable Rights, that among these are life, liberty and the pursuit of happiness and that the purpose of our government is to secure these rights. That means that you have a right to be free, and that your government is accountable to guarantee your freedom. The promise of freedom, of the opportunity to be and become whomever you want to be, has brought waves of immigrants to these shores for two centuries.

We can debate all day long about how this or that government policy limits our freedom, but one thing is beyond argument: you can *give away* your liberty and opportunity. Too many Americans have frittered away their freedom through indebtedness. Debt steals possibility from your future. We no longer toss debtors into prison, but many of us are living in a prison of our own making. It is a gilded cage: a couple of really cool cars or trucks, granite counter tops in the kitchen, a closet full shoes "that are to die for." The availability of easy credit, starting right out of high school, leads to lives of indentured service: not to a merchant or farmer but to banks and mortgage companies. Too many people can never become what they want to be because they are shackled to paying for what they are.

If losing your job teaches you nothing else, I hope that it teaches you the folly of chaining yourself to large consumer debts while living paycheck to paycheck.

You have the right, as an American, to be free from self-imposed debt. You may have become overly dependent on your job. Now don't get me wrong, I'm not saying that you don't need to work for money. I'm not telling you to move to a cabin in the woods, wear animal skins and grow your own turnips. Nor am I suggesting that we all should work for low-paying non-profits or go overseas and be missionaries. But many of us—maybe you—might want to change jobs for a variety of reasons: location, vocation, to take a risk to advance or to downsize and go back to school, to start a business, whatever. If we are tied to an overvalued house and a pile of consumer debt, we can't afford to risk our direct-deposited paychecks. The irony is that the more risks we take with our spending, the less risks we can take with our work. Now unemployment has brought the ugly truth to the surface: we *really needed that job.*

Some people in this position expect the government to bail them out. All of a sudden it has dawned on them that they aren't free: their house is worth less than they owe on the mortgage and equity lines that they tacked onto it, and that doesn't even include the cars, credit cards and all the rest. They look at those words in the Declaration of Independence and demand that the government make good on their right to liberty by pushing their debt onto those who aren't trapped... yet. What they are really doing is stealing some freedom from neighbors who more wisely preserved theirs. That wasn't the promise of the Declaration, but the politics will play out however they play out.

You, however, can begin taking advantage of your right to liberty now. How? It's pretty simple: from this point on, *don't spend more than you make.* Live below your means, not above or even right at them. Start getting rid of your debt as fast as possible and avoid any new debt like a coiled rattlesnake in the corner of your tent. There are times and reasons to borrow money, but they should be few and far between in life. This is not a debt management or financial planning book, but get one and start following its advice. Again, I strongly recommend anything by Dave Ramsey.

Living below your means instead of above them gives you freedom in your job search. It makes it possible for you to take a lower paying job because it is more interesting to you or is in a better location or offers the possibility to advance down the line, etc. It makes starting your own business more feasible. It allows you to consider career changes or short-term work projects as a sub-contractor. It certainly makes it easier to survive through economic cycles. I'm not suggesting that you curtail your ambitions at all: if you dream of making a million dollars a year, then just plan to live on half a million (that shouldn't be too tough). If you make fifty grand, can you live on forty?

Beyond reducing debt and spending less than you make, you can hold onto your freedom by paying more attention to *micro*-economies than to *macro*-economies. Macro-economies are the big cycles: the national and global financial markets, international trade, the fate of huge corporations--the things that we hear about on the news and all have opinions about, but also the things that you have no direct control over. By contrast, micro-economies are small networks of commerce and trade. Leading up to the Panic of 1819 and so many of the recessions since then, people gambled their time and money on the big cycles of the macro-economy. You have much more control over your own micro-economy. Where will you live and how much will you pay for that? Can you buy a duplex, live in one half and rent the other out to minimize your housing costs? Can you work your life out so that you can walk to work or minimize your commute? Can you negotiate with your employer to be a sub-contractor in return for other advantages like working from home? Can your family start a small business? Where will you shop? Can you join or form purchasing cooperatives to negotiate better terms for things that you buy or need? Can you engage in house-swaps for vacations? Can you buy a rental house for the old fashioned reason of putting tenants in it and generating a revenue stream, not to "flip?" Sure, you'll have to fix toilets and collect rent, but you'll also have more control than you would speculating.

One type of micro-economy that I've mentioned before is bartering networks. You can work out a straight barter arrangement between families to reduce expenses (I'll clean your house if you cut my kid's hair), or factor trade into small business exchanges (my real estate agent will reduce his commission if my web-design business makes improvements in his site). In the companion workbook to *The ReExamined Life* I talk more about building and investing in your own micro-economy, but the goal is to take control of whatever you can, wherever you can, to preserve as much freedom as possible so that you can live your life without dependency on employers, financial markets or government.

The Right to the Pursuit of Happiness

In July, 1776 the Continental Congress asked Jefferson to write a "declaration of independence." He drew heavily on two sources for the passage on rights: the *Virginia Declaration of Rights,* written by George Mason a month earlier, and English philosopher John Locke's *Second Treatise on Government.* What's interesting is that in both those sources the emphasis was not on the "life, liberty and the pursuit of happiness," but on life, liberty and *property.* Most of the founders believed that governments should guarantee and guard the concept of private property (whether that's real estate or a comic book collection). In his first draft Jefferson substituted the phrase *"pursuit of happiness"* for *"property"* as the third right that the Creator gives and for which governments are implemented to defend.

Government gives you a right to *pursue* happiness, not to *be* happy. It is not supposed to even out all our outcomes, to make sure that everyone gets the same rewards in life regardless of talent, choices, opportunity or effort. The genius of America is that it gives you the right to be a fool and a right to fail.

My advice to you, after you have lost your job, is to claim that right to pursue happiness. Do not depend on or expect anyone else—not employers, financial markets, politicians or government bureaucracies—to provide your happiness. Heed this warning: if you believe that the government or other institutions exist to give you a right to happiness, to provide it for you, then *they will determine what that happiness is.* They will hand you whatever it is that they are selling and say, "Here. Be happy with this. Now say, 'Thank you.'" It might be government handouts, a government house or a government health plan. Or it might be a corporation, with all its benefits and perks, that you are trusting to take care of you. Please listen: whoever is guaranteeing your happiness decides what it will be.

Jefferson went out of his way in his first draft of the Declaration of Independence to make the point that the government exists to give you a right to pursue whatever it is that you decide will make you happy. That might be inventing the Next Greatest Thing or playing with it. It might be making a fortune or living like a hobo, raising a family in the suburbs or performing as a street mime in Times Square. You get to choose and you get to assume the rights and risks of that pursuit.

After you've lost your job you might be tempted to demand that someone give you a new one. You might be tempted to listen to those who tell you that you have a right to a job and a nice house in the suburbs, that you have a right not to fail. But there is a terrible cost: if you give away your right to fail you will give away your right to succeed, to pursue happiness as *you* define it.

I said at the beginning of this book that I hoped that some of you would try to launch global corporations from your garage, invent great things or make obscenely large fortunes-- maybe all of the above. I really do hope that some of you will, because our country and our world desperately need your achievement. But I would be remiss if I didn't close this book by re- minding you that pursuing money *for its own sake* is what got a lot of us into trouble. Capit- alism is the most effective engine to drive growth and prosperity and justice that history has ever seen, and as the economist Adam Smith said, the profit motive is like an "invisible hand," that guides free markets, creating wealth and oppor- tunity and jobs and all the miracles and wonders of technology.

But hopefully your passion isn't money for its own sake. Hopefully you are motivated to achieve because of the valuable things that you can do with the money you earn. Cheap money, money that you don't really work for, brings very little genuine happiness. Think that's an anti-capitalist statement? Not at all, because many millionaires and billionaires enjoy their money as a happy consequence of a productive life. Contrast that with lottery winners. Too many people who win the big jackpot just blow it, and many end up miserable. It's wealth disconnected from achievement or value: just a lot of stuff dumped on someone without the character to appreciate it. The same thing could be said for trust funders at one end of the economic ladder and those who grow up on welfare at the other. Money, *just money,* disconnected from value, is nothing but trouble. Consider chapter 5, verses 10-11 of the Old Testament Book of Ecclesiastes:

Whoever loves money never has money enough; whoever loves wealth is never satisfied with his income. This too is meaningless. As goods increase, so do those who consume them. And what benefit are they to the owner except to feast his eyes on them?

Pursue happiness. It's your right as an American citizen. Don't depend on anyone else for it, and don't let anyone tell you what it should be. Some of you, in pursuing happiness, will do things so useful to the rest of us that you will make a pile of money. Good for you, but all that money will be the fruit of a happy pursuit, not the object.

•　　•　　•

Irony is a ruthless thing. Thomas Jefferson —the writer of the Declaration of Independence, the president who made the Louisiana Purchase, the ex-president who had warned throughout the 1810s that America was in a bubble economy and had exchanged the virtues of 1776 for an age of speculators—was one of the victims of the Panic of 1819. For a number of reasons, Jefferson had always struggled to keep his beloved plantation Monticello profitable. But when the depression began in 1819 he was as hard hit as anyone else. When he died on Fourth of July in 1826 (ironically on the fiftieth anniversary of the Declaration and the same day as his co-author John Adams), he died deeply in debt. His home, his possessions and his entire estate was sold at auction by his creditors.

The other day I heard someone say that that he feels stupid because the current recession has left him in such financial difficulty. If only he had been smarter, he said, he might have avoided this fate.

My friend is a bright guy, but he's not as smart as Thomas Jefferson. For all of his intelligence and his capacity to pen the words about unalienable rights to life, liberty and the pursuit of happiness Jefferson didn't escape history's cruel wheel.

We may not be able to avoid the wars, famines, plagues, disasters and economic cycles of this world. But the best guide that we have through it all is not necessarily intelligence. It's something that the ancient Hebrews called *hokmah,* which the Bible translates as "wisdom." It's a sort of God-given street-smarts, a pattern of life that is prudent and clever, righteous and healthy. You could manage a hedge fund, perform brain surgery or design a space craft and still not have *hokmah,* wisdom. The person who has it may or may not get rich; their house may or may not get hit by a tornado; they may or may not lose their job when the corporation they work for goes bankrupt. But the wise person, the person with *hokmah,* always seems to have their life on a solid foundation. Their relationships, their life, their marriage, family, friendships, health and heart always seem to roll with the punches, to survive whatever life throws at them. Despite history, despite circumstances, their pattern of life is unshakable and they always find a way to do and be well in the end.

I called this book *The ReExamined Life: What is Possible after Job Loss?* We've seen lots of things that are possible, but I'd like to end by suggesting just one more. It's possible for you to become wise, to use this moment of crisis to rebuild your life on a new foundation. You can read all about it in the Book of Proverbs. You could do worse than to go forward basing your future career on what is written there. In the first chapter the author, Solomon, says that Proverbs is useful...

for attaining wisdom and discipline; for un-

derstanding words of insight; for acquiring a disciplined and prudent life, doing what is right and just and fair; for giving prudence to the simple, knowledge and discretion to the young- let the wise listen and add to their learning, and let the discerning get guidance...The fear of the LORD is the beginning of knowledge, but fools despise wisdom and discipline.

The Next Greatest Generation

T hrough this book we've explored ways to recover and reorder your career. More than that, we've talked about how reordering your career is an opportunity to reorder your life. As the book's title says, we've seen that reexamining your life after losing your job makes it possible to not just work for a living, but to work for a life *worth* living.

What if you weren't the only one to do that? What if lots of us used this current economic downturn as an opportunity to start working and spending and investing differently? What if lots of us rethought our values and our priorities and our expectations? What if lots of us saw liberty as not only the right to read or watch or worship whatever we want but as freedom from debt and dependency? What if lots of us created something of real value with our work? What if lots of us earned and spent our money and time with more wisdom and deliberate choice? What would be the cumulative effect of that?

There's a lot of talk today about the Great Depression. Some say that we're either in the worst economy since then or slipping into another one. By the time this book is published or read, those predictions may have come true or may have been fears that didn't materialize. Regardless, Americans have a strange love-hate fascination with the Great Depression. It frightens us for the obvious reasons. Still, we wax poetic about the values that America learned and the generation that it produced.

The Depression-era family which loves each other through tough times, holds onto simple things and makes do with less is a staple of American film, television and books. The father who loses his successful job or business and is reduced to some hard, menial labor which he does with dignity to support his family is the hero of many American histories and legends. We are proud that young American men raised during the Depression passed the tests of character on the beaches of Normandy and Iwo Jima. Tom Brokaw called them "the Greatest Generation."

We love the *idea* of the values that they learned but not necessarily the values themselves. The actual lessons pounded into them during the 1930s were about hard work without shortcuts, about frugality, about distrust of banks, get-rich-quick-schemes and fancy "investment vehicles." They kept cash for a rainy day in a coffee can on the top shelf of the linen closet; they bought houses to live in or rent out, not to "flip"; they went to work like they went off to World War II: for the duration. They gave more to charity than their children did, who have *talked* more about charity. They didn't expect or demand success, back-slaps, congratulations or equal outcomes for everyone. When they voted in the presidential election of 1960, during their mid to late thirties, they elected one of their own (albeit one who had come from wealth) who said to them in his inaugural address, "Ask not what your country can do for you -- ask what you can do for your country." Then they put a man on the moon in ten years.

All of this gets lost in something of a nostalgic fog. Many of us actually found our parents and grandparents annoying when they raised their eyebrows at how we lived and worked and spent. We told ourselves, and sometimes them, that they didn't understand that this was a new decade or a new century. We snickered because they didn't "get" our generation and we figured they just weren't clever enough to understand how work was done or money was made these days.

Their children and grandchildren (that would be us) have gotten ourselves into a fine mess. We bought more than we could afford, learned few transferable skills and expect, nay *demand*, our economy to grow at a 3-5% annual rate, and we track that *per quarter.* Many of us believe that we are entitled to not only an ever-rising standard of living, but one that rises continually without plateaus or hiccups. If it doesn't, if we face a quarter or two or three of contraction or even slow growth, we look for someone to blame. In our last few presidential elections politicians have worked hard to capture the *theater and rhetoric* of Kennedy, but their campaign platforms and promises have inverted the whole point of his Greatest Generation formula: we ask what our country can do for us. So we are passing the Greatest Debt in history on to the next generation to bail us out. We consider ourselves, to use the ironic euphemism of the government bail-out, "too big to fail." Despite our nostalgia about them, we are terrified, absolutely knock-kneed and night-sweats terrified, of going through what the Greatest Generation went through.

As Britain prepared for the Nazi onslaught during World War II, after years of suffering through the Depression themselves, Winston Churchill spoke to Parliament of his determination that the present crisis would not destroy them. "Let us therefore brace ourselves to our duties, and so bear ourselves that, if the British Empire and its Commonwealth lasts for a thousand years, men will still say, '*This was their finest hour!*'"

What if lots of us used this moment in our nation's history, whether it turns out to be a once-in-a-century depression or merely a once-in-a-generation recession, as a once-in–a-lifetime opportunity for reexamination? Reexamination of what we thought that we knew about why and how we work and spend. Are we working for a living or for a life *worth* living?

Perhaps, if enough of us did that, this crisis could be our finest hour. We could raise another Great Generation: one that recaptures a way of living, working, saving and spending that made the United States of America, as Ronald Reagan said during another dark moment in our economic history, a "shining city on a hill," a land of opportunity and invention and freedom and prosperity that the whole world admired. That would be something worth working for, maybe even worth sacrificing for.

❧ About the Author ❧

Bill van Steenis has been an executive recruiter since the 1980's. In 1992 he founded Prosource Executive Search, and has seen the employment landscape change through many business cycles, recessions and industrial shifts.

Bill resides in Holland, Michigan and Orlando, Forida.

Made in the USA